You Can Do It!

Susan and Matt —
It's always a pleasure to
see you all in Bethany Beach —
I hope you find the book to be
helpful.
More information is on my
web site —

WWW.FINANCIALSECURITYGUIDE.COM

Dan

You Can Do It!

An Easy Step-By-Step Guide to Financial Security

Donald H Young

iUniverse, Inc.
New York   Bloomington

You Can Do It!
An Easy Step-By-Step Guide to Financial Security

iUniverse books may be ordered through booksellers or by contacting:

iUniverse
1663 Liberty Drive
Bloomington, IN 47403
www.iuniverse.com
1-800-Authors (1-800-288-4677)

ISBN: 978-0-595-48979-4 (pbk)
ISBN: 978-0-595-60916-1 (ebk)
ISBN: 978-0-595-48966-4 (cloth)

Printed in the United States of America

iUniverse rev. date: 1/7/09

This book is dedicated to the following members of my family—my wife, Karen, who encouraged me to write this book and was so supportive while I was working on it; our sons, Rob and Ryan, of whom we will always be extremely proud and who represent our enduring legacy; and my parents, Ellen and Don Young, who provided tremendous educational and developmental opportunities for me.

This book is also dedicated to each of you. I have recently retired from forty years in the institutional investment management business. At the time of my retirement, I was responsible for a business that had $23 billion in assets under management for three hundred clients around the world and a staff of fifty-five. My objective in writing this book is to give something back to you by sharing some of what I have learned and helping you apply it to build a personal financial management structure that is simple, durable, comprehensive, and responsive to your objectives.

CONTENTS

Introduction

A journey of a thousand miles begins with a single step.

Confucius

Many people either have not thought much about the issues involved with personal financial management (PFM) or are not satisfied with the efforts they have made so far. Such key functions as setting objectives, managing cash flows, building and managing a balance sheet, budgeting, planning for retirement, structuring an investment program, and preparing and maintaining critical documents have not been a high priority. As a result, most people find themselves caught up in a repeating cycle of frustration.

They sense that a better job could be done, and they are always trying to get better organized to do it. However, most do not succeed, which results in renewed attempts that also fail. This creates more confusion and frustration, and so the cycle keeps repeating, and people finally give up. If you are one of these individuals, this book will guide you in a systematic way to achieve your PFM goals.

In my opinion, the lack of satisfaction is not because most people do not care about these issues. In fact, they do care, and they would like to address them. However, it is unfortunate that they have not been able to accomplish as much as they want or as much as they could with proper planning. Why is this?

There are many reasons why people do not have the structure and control of their PFM system that they desire, including the following:

- The process of developing it appears to be overwhelming.
- A low level of understanding exists about exactly what needs to be done to develop a PFM structure and how to do it.
- There are not clearly stated objectives.
- Many people do not involve themselves in the development process and take personal responsibility for it and its results. Counting on friends, neighbors, stock brokers, and insurance agents to do this for you is no substitute.
- There is a failure to recognize that, while developing and maintaining a PFM system is attainable for almost everyone, the path to success cannot be followed haphazardly, any more than driving from Chicago to New York can. What is needed is a PFM plan, which is an organized and rigorous process that requires considerable effort at the outset and consists of a number of specific steps that have to be addressed. In general, once the personal investment has been made to develop and follow this plan, the incremental effort is much smaller and principally concerned with maintenance. Developing and implementing this plan is one of the most important projects a person can undertake.
- People choose the wrong vehicles and individuals to implement whatever structure they establish.
- There is often an inability to keep the long term in mind, and the result is that people get thrown off track by short-term developments.

To many, some of these reasons for failure to develop a PFM plan may seem intimidating and difficult to overcome. However, I can assure you that all of them can be addressed by simply focusing on a limited number of things that need to be accomplished in a very straightforward way. On the other hand, there is almost an infinite number of things, the most important of which I will point out, which can distract you and contribute to a failure to reach your objectives.

Therefore, it is the purpose of this book to help you weave together the basic principles of personal finance into a PFM plan and to show you how to avoid the pitfalls that can either keep you from developing the plan in the first place or keep you from achieving it once you have it in place. This book will help you develop and implement successfully your own PFM plan.

This is not the most sophisticated book you could read on this subject or the most specialized discussion of any of the primary subjects I will address. However, it may be that the sophistication of many books, the astounding number and bewildering variety of books on this subject, and the focus on specialization in many cases have led to a collective failure to make people feel that they are in control of their financial situations. They are so confused that they are paralyzed into doing nothing. This book provides a simple, comprehensive blueprint for setting and achieving your objectives.

In the interest of full disclosure, I want you to know at the outset that I have biases in favor of standard approaches rather than exotic solutions (i.e., keep it simple); low fees; investment vehicles that provide the performance of the assets they represent with very little deviation; financial building blocks that directly address particular problems and not several others at the same time; organizations and individuals that have high ethical standards and do not have conflicts of interest with you; diversification (spreading your assets across several investments) as opposed to concentration; and personal involvement and commitment by you rather than reliance primarily on others. This book is for those who are committed to make the effort to "own" their PFM plan.

Given the diversity of personal situations and objectives, it cannot, of course, be my purpose to make choices for you. Only you can do that. However, what I will try to do is to point out what the available choices are and to provide some guidance on how to make the right choices among them.

As indicated in the table of contents, the book is organized into six parts:
- Part I provides basic background information that will be helpful in understanding the rest of the book. Chapters 1 and 2 introduce two important concepts—compound interest, and investment return and risk.

- Part II deals with the critical issue of setting personal objectives. Chapter 3 shows you how to establish objectives for your personal financial management.
- Part III covers three basic areas of personal financial management. Chapter 4 provides a simple and easy-to-implement structure for managing your cash flows. The role of money market funds and the importance of credit ratings are also discussed.

  Chapters 5 and 6 discuss how to create two essential personal management tools—a personal balance sheet and a budget. Part of the financial management process is very much like managing a business—your business—and these are the basic tools of business management.

  Chapter 5 shows you how to create a balance sheet so that you can determine your assets, liabilities, and personal net worth, and manage them effectively.

  Chapter 6 shows how to create a budget and a tracking system to determine how you are doing relative to what you want to accomplish.
- Part IV addresses the important issue of insurance. Chapter 7 outlines the important decisions that have to be made to ensure that you are properly protected by insurance—health, life, and liability.
- Part V outlines how to address planning for retirement, and it consists of four chapters. Chapters 8, 9, 10, and 11 should be considered as a group, because they represent a step-by-step approach to retirement planning. Chapter 8 shows you how to estimate what income you will need in retirement and from what sources you might expect to get it.

  Chapter 9 presents a methodology for calculating what total assets will be needed at retirement to produce the required income in retirement and how this sum of assets might be created.

  Chapter 10 focuses on required returns from assets and how to select assets for your long-term investment programs.

  Finally, chapter 11 describes how to put together long-term investment programs for pre-retirement, retirement, and college saving.
- Part VI consists of chapter 12, which outlines an extensive array of critical documents you will need to prepare and update on a regular basis, including living wills, arrangements for guardianship of minor children, trusts, and the designation of powers of attorney and health care proxies.
- The Conclusion provides a brief summary of the entire book.

This is not the journey of a thousand miles to which Confucius refers. However, it is a journey, and it does begin with a single step. That step is to make a commitment to invest your time and effort to develop a PFM plan. The alternative of continuing to do no more than you are doing today is not very attractive for most people, and it could prove to be extremely costly in the long term in terms of opportunities lost and failure to achieve your objectives. I hope this book will make your journey easier so that the chances that you will reach your destination are dramatically improved.

I would like to thank all of my close associates at the various firms within which we built the Invesco Global Structured Products Group—Citibank, USF&G, Chancellor Capital Management, LGT Asset Management, and Invesco—particularly Chuck DuBois, Stuart Kaye, and Jerry Lefkowitz. I am grateful to all of them for the learning opportunities and support they provided. I would also like to thank my associate, Marlyne Page, for her invaluable assistance in various techniques I used to prepare this book. It has been a privilege to work with all of them.

I would also like to thank my wife, Karen, our two sons, Robert and Ryan, and the many friends who read and commented on this book as it was being written. These people include, but are not limited to, Stanley Durkee, Jerry Lefkowitz, and Above & Beyond, whose expertise in word processing created the first-draft manuscript.

Don Young
Upper Montclair, New Jersey
January 2008

PART I

Basic Background

Chapter 1

Understanding the Magic of Compound Interest

The most powerful force in the universe is compound interest.

Attributed to Albert Einstein

As Einstein suggests, compound interest is one of the most important financial management tools of all time, and that is why I am devoting an entire chapter to making sure that you have a good understanding of what it is and how it can be used to help you achieve your objectives.

How does it work? Figure 1.1 shows an example of the principal types of information involved in compound interest. The first is the investment amount, sometimes called the principal, which in this case is $10,000. The second is the annual interest rate, also known as the investment rate of return, which is 5%. The final important input is the number of years during which the investment amount is earning interest, which is also called the term of the investment. In figure 1.1, the term is one year.

Figure 1.1
Example Data for Compound Interest

Investment Amount	$10,000
Annual Interest Rate	5%
Number of Years of Investment	1

Note that the annual interest rate of 5% shown in figure 1.1 is equal to 5/100, or 0.05. That is, 5% translated into its decimal equivalent is 0.05; 10%, or 10/100, translated into its decimal equivalent is 0.10. For some of the figures in this book, I will use the decimal equivalent of percent.

The result of investing $10,000 at 5% for one year is shown in figure 1.2.

Figure 1.2
Results at the End of Year 1

	Beginning	Ending
Original Investment Amount	$10,000	$10,000
Interest Received (= $10,000 X 0.05)		$500
Total Ending Investment Amount		$10,500

At the end of the year, you have the original $10,000 with which you started, but you also have an additional $500, which represents the interest on $10,000 at 5%. The total value of your investment at the end of year one (the total ending investment amount) is $10,500. The way to calculate the ending value of your investment without using figure 1.2 is to multiply the original investment amount by (1 plus the interest rate in decimals), or (1 plus 0.05), or (1.05): $10,000 times 1.05 equals $10,500.

It is relatively easy to understand the calculation for one year. It is when multiple years are considered that the magic of compound interest becomes clear.

In figure 1.3, the data from the first year of figure 1.2 are repeated. The starting investment for year two is the ending investment for year one. Figure 1.3 is based on the assumptions shown in figure 1.1.

Figure 1.3
Compound Interest—Multiple Years

Year	Starting Investment	Interest on Original Investment	Interest on Interest	Ending Investment
1	$10,000	$500		$10,500
2	$10,500	$500	$25	$11,025

As you can see, you still get the same interest, or $500, on the same investment amount, or $10,000. However, note that there is a new column, which is entitled "interest on interest." This is the interest you receive in year two on the interest you received in year one. The ending investment for year two can also be determined by multiplying the starting investment amount of $10,500 by the same 1.05 that was used in figure 1.1 to get the ending value at the end of year one.

The bottom line at the end of year two is that you have $25 more in investment value than you would expect to have after receiving interest of $500 for each of two years, because of the compounding effect of earning interest on interest.

In figure 1.4, the data from the two years shown in figure 1.3 are repeated. However, eight more years have been added, for a total of ten. The calculations for each of the additional eight years are exactly the same as the calculation for year two. That is, to get the ending investment amount for a particular year, you multiply the investment amount at the end of the previous year by 1.05.

Figure 1.4
Compound Interest—Multiple Years

Year	Starting Investment	Interest on Original Investment	Interest on Interest	Ending Investment
				$10,000
1	$10,000	$500		10,500
2	10,500	500	$25	11,025
3	11,025	500	51	11,576
4	11,576	500	79	12,155
5	12,155	500	108	12,763
6	12,763	500	138	13,401
7	13,401	500	170	14,071
8	14,071	500	204	14,775
9	14,775	500	238	15,513
10	$15,513	$500	$276	$16,289
Total		$5,000	$1,289	

Note that the interest on the original investment amount for the ten-year period is $500 times 10, or $5,000, as you would expect. The really important observation is that you have received an additional $1,289 in interest, because of the compounding effect of interest on interest. In short, because of compounding, you have almost 26% more in interest.

Without compound interest, your ending investment amount would have been $15,000 (the $10,000 starting investment amount plus $5,000 in interest). However, the ending value of the original investment amount is now $16,289, which is more than 8% more than you would have had ($15,000) without the effect of compounding interest on interest.

This is a truly amazing result, and what is more amazing is that you do not have to do anything to get this result other than making the original investment and keeping it invested at an interest rate of 5% for the full ten years.

Another example of the effect of compound interest will illustrate its power. Let me ask you a question: "which alternative would give you the most money at age 65?"

- Alternative A
  - Receive annual payments of $10,000 every year from age 21 through age 35 (fifteen years), a total of $150,000.
  - Receive no additional payments after age 35.
  - Earn an interest rate of 5%.

- Alternative B
  - Receive annual payments of $10,000 every year from age 36 through age 65 (thirty years), a total of $300,000.
  - Earn an interest rate of 5%.

Note that the payments in Alternative A only last for fifteen years, and at the end of that time you receive only interest at 5% for the next thirty years. In Alternative B, payments do not start until age 36, but they last for thirty years—twice as long as the period of payments in Alternative A.

The results are shown in figure 1.5.

**Figure 1.5
Ending Amounts
for
Alternatives A and B**

Alternative	Cumulative Payments	Interest	Ending Amount
Alternative A at Age 35	$150,000	$76,575	$226,575
Alternative A at Age 65	$150,000	$829,244	$979,244
Alternative B	$300,000	$397,608	$697,608

This is an astonishing result. Even though you get payments for half as long and payments stop at age 35, you end up with significantly more money at age 65 with Alternative A, which is $979,244, than in Alternative B, which is $697,608. This is because the value you accumulate by age 35 of $226,575 gives you such a head start that, even though you do not receive any more payments, the compounding of this amount at 5% keeps you well ahead of Alternative B. Look at the difference in interest income over the respective periods.

Incidentally, Alternative A gives you more money at age 65 than Alternative B at any compounding interest rate in excess of 3%. For example, at an 8% interest rate, you would have almost $3 million at age 65 with Alternative A, compared to only $1.2 million with Alternative B.

The two important conclusions from this example are: (1) the more money you can put to work, the better it is for you, and (2) the earlier you can put your money to work, the longer the period you will have to benefit from compound interest.

Of course, stopping payments at age 35 is arbitrary and only appropriate for this example. What would the ending value at 65 for Alternative A be if, instead of stopping at age 35, you continued to receive payments of $10,000 every year from age 36 through age 65? I will call this Alternative C. The results are shown in figure 1.6, which also includes the data shown in figure 1.5 for comparison.

Figure 1.6
Ending Amounts
for
Alternatives A and B

Alternative	Cumulative Payments	Interest	Ending Amount
Alternative A at Age 35	$150,000	$76,575	$226,575
Alternative A at Age 65	$150,000	$829,244	$979,244
Alternative B	$300,000	$397,608	$697,608
Alternative C	$450,000	$1,226,852	$1,676,852

The lesson from figure 1.6 is that if you could continue to receive payments after age 35, you would have approximately $700,000 more at age 65, as shown for Alternative C, than in Alternative A.

You can now see what a powerful tool compound interest can be. The best thing about it is that it requires very little effort on your part, other than making sure that you are as exposed to it as early as possible in your life and that you stay exposed to it. Furthermore, it does not cost you anything. Thus, it is the closest thing to a "free lunch" that you will ever find in the financial world, and there is no reason not to maximize your exposure to it.

Finally, to see the magnitude of the compounding effect over long periods of time, it is essential to separate the ending value of $1,676,852 from figure 1.6 at age 65 into its components. This breakdown is provided in figure 1.7.

Figure 1.7
Breakdown of Ending Value for Alternative C

Total Annual Payments	$450,000
Total Simple Interest	$517,500
Total Compound Interest	$709,352
Total Investment Value	$1,676,852

Figure 1.7 shows the ultimate in the magic of compound interest. At age 65, total payments for Alternative C would amount to $10,000 per year times forty-five years, or $450,000. Simple interest, ignoring compounding of interest on interest, would amount to $517,500. What is extraordinary is that interest on interest—the compounding effect—would have contributed $709,352, a figure well in excess of either the total payments or the simple interest.

An amazing 42% of the ending value would have been created by compound interest. At the beginning of this chapter, I indicated that compound interest is one of the strongest financial management mechanisms of all time. Hopefully, at this point, you can see why.

The figures in this chapter assume that you receive payments of $10,000 per year over some period from someone and invest them at 5%. Of course, the effect is the same if you were investing these amounts yourself out of your own resources. However, most people probably did not start at age 21 in Alternative A and probably could not invest that much at that point in any case. The ages and the amounts are used simply for illustrative purposes.

Nevertheless, even if you did not start at age 21 with an annual payment of $10,000, it is never too late to start. Compound interest works whenever you start and with whatever amount you can afford. The only differences would be that the period of the investment would not be as long as the period on which these examples are based and the ending amounts would not be as large.

I am sure it has occurred to you that exposure to compound interest can be both positive and negative. All of the examples discussed so far in this chapter indicate how a positive exposure to compound interest can be used to your advantage. What is a negative exposure? A negative exposure to compound interest is created when you borrow money, do not pay it back right away, and the lender charges you interest. In this case, your negative exposure is the reverse side of your lender's positive exposure to you.

In many cases, such as a mortgage, your negative exposure is built into your payment schedule, and it is appropriate and necessary. You simply could not come up with the purchase price of your home on your own. However, in the case of credit card debt, which is basically discretionary, if you do not pay off your monthly balance, the 15% to 20% annual interest rates charged by the credit card companies compound against you (this might be called "reverse compounding"). This situation is illustrated in figure 1.8.

Figure 1.8
Reverse Compounding

Assumptions

Original Credit Card Debt $10,000
Annual Minimum Required Payment $1,200
Annual Interest Rate   15%

Result after Five Years

Credit Card Debt Outstanding $10,809

You start out with credit card debt of $10,000, and you make the minimum payment required by the credit card company. I assume for this example that the minimum payment is $100 per month, or $1,200 per year. Many families pay the minimum because they are unable to pay any more, but to be in that position is a very bad idea. The interest rate is 15% per year. How much will your credit card debt be at the end of five years?

You might think that it would be lower than the original amount of $10,000, because you have made payments that total $6,000 ($1,200 per year times five years). However, as figure 1.8 illustrates, by the end of five years, you will owe about $10,800. You now owe more than the amount with which you started. This really should not be an astounding result now that you understand compound interest, but you can see that the effect of reverse compounding can conceivably be devastating.

If the same situation continues for another five years, the credit card debt outstanding will have grown to $12,436, a 24% increase from where you started. This negative exposure to compound interest can quickly mount up and create a disastrous financial situation for you before you know it. If you are in this position, you are clearly going in the wrong direction.

Therefore, negative exposure to compound interest is something you should desperately strive to avoid. Unlike the situation with the mortgage, this is a position you can avoid by not creating more credit card debt than you can pay off every month. I will show you how to do this in chapter 6, which discusses how to put together and live within a budget.

You must decide which side of compound interest you want to be on. Do you want to have compound interest working for you to build assets over time, or do you want to constantly conduct a losing battle with the effects of compound interest working against you? The answer should be clear.

Note that there are two specific problems with the second alternative: (1) your credit card debt will continue to grow, creating more and more of a problem as time goes by, and (2) you will suffer a tremendous opportunity cost from not having compound interest working for you, which will significantly compromise your ability to achieve your long-term financial goals.

Now that you understand compound interest and how it works, the question is, how can you put this powerful financial tool to work for you? This question will be addressed in chapters 8–11, which outline how to use it to achieve your long-term financial goals.

Bottom Line

- There are only three things involved with compound interest: the investment amount, the interest rate, and the length of the investment.
- The magic of compound interest is that you receive interest on interest, and this amount can add significantly to your return on investment over time.
- Benefiting from the extraordinary power of compound interest requires almost no effort on your part, except to expose yourself to it. It is the closest thing to a "free lunch" that you will ever find in the financial world.
- Investing as much as you can as early as you can dramatically increases the value you will have at the end of any investment period, as compared to delaying getting started with your investment program.
- Make sure that compound interest works for you.
- Desperately avoid being exposed to reverse compounding.

Chapter 2

Learning about Investment Return and Risk

Our favorite holding period is forever.

Warren Buffett
Legendary Investor

A critical assumption in the compound interest examples in the previous chapter is that the interest rate, or the investment return, being compounded is constant. This is a useful assumption for the purpose of understanding the essentials of compound interest.

However, while a constant compounding rate is available for some investments, it definitely is not for others. The objective of this chapter is to describe the potential returns for key investment assets, to outline the possible variations in these returns, and to explain how to think about variable compounding rates.

The basic asset classes that should be your principal focus as you develop an investment program designed to meet your long-term financial objectives are cash investments, bonds or fixed income (these assets are referred to as fixed income, because they generally pay an amount of interest that is fixed), stocks, and real estate.

There is a bewilderingly large number of subsets of these basic assets. For example, for stocks, there are domestic versus foreign stocks, growth versus value stocks, and small versus large stocks. For fixed income, there are U.S. government bonds, municipal bonds, corporate bonds, and high yield bonds, among others. What makes fixed income even more confusing is that all of these types of bonds have terms that range from short to long. Then, there are other very specialized assets, such as hedge funds, commodities, and gold, which fall outside of the four basic asset classes.

The problem with the subsets and the specialized assets is that, while they are exotic and interesting conversation items, with few exceptions, they are not critical to solving the most basic problem of asset allocation among long-term investment assets, which you inevitably have and which will be discussed in chapters 8–11.

In fact, attempting to deal with these subsets and the specialized assets is one of those distractions to which I referred in the Introduction and which you should avoid. Trying to determine how to invest in the four basic asset classes is hard enough. Losing focus by getting involved outside of them will lead you astray. As a result, this book will not deal with them.

This chapter, then, is about return and risk for these four basic asset classes. Return is a fairly easy concept to understand. At one point, you have an investment value, and at another point, you have a different investment value. Dividing the ending value by the beginning value and taking into account the period of time over which the investment was made allows you to calculate a return for the investment. If you started with an investment of $1,000 and you ended with an investment of $2,000 ten years later, you can determine that the compound annual rate of return is 7.2%.

However, risk is more complicated. Risk can be defined either as: (1) the variability of returns for an investment around a long-term trend line (this is usually referred to as "relative risk," because you are concerned about how closely an investment return tracks the trend line), or (2) the probability of loss of a certain amount for an investment (this is usually referred to as "absolute risk"). Both are important, particularly the probability of loss. People react much more negatively to actual loss than they react favorably to unrealized gains.

The first definition of risk has to do with the possible variability on an annual basis of a return like the 7.2% indicated above. Though 7.2% is the compound return over the ten-year period, that does not mean that the return is 7.2% every year. The question that this definition of risk addresses is how good or how bad could the return be in a particular year during that period.

In other words, what is the variability of that 7.2% return in any one year? The answer might be that the annual return should fall within a range of 2% to 12% two years out of three over this period. This range gives you a sense of how variable the returns actually might be, and you can make a judgment about whether such a potential risk experience is acceptable.

The second definition of risk, which is related to the first, addresses how much money you can lose over a particular time frame of interest. What is the absolute loss of investment value that you may experience with a particular asset over a particular time period? Five percent? Twenty percent? Fifty percent?

Notwithstanding the attractiveness of a long-term investment, if you think that you might lose 50% of your investment value in a short period of time, such as one to two years, and if this would cause a great deal of discomfort, then it would make sense not to have 100% of your portfolio exposed to this investment.

Since, in most cases, the downside risk can be seen in the analysis of the variability of possible returns, this chapter will focus on the first definition of risk—the variability of annual returns around a compound return over a particular time frame.

Cash Investments

A cash investment, the first of the basic asset classes mentioned above, is a reserve asset, in the sense that it should be available for a rainy day, or it is something into which you put your money when you are hesitant to invest in something else. Cash investments include money market funds, certificates of deposit, and savings accounts. These are considered to be investments, because when you make them you expect to earn a return. This is not true, for example, of cash that is saved under the mattress, which earns nothing.

The return on cash investments, or the compounding rate, varies with short-term interest rates in the marketplace, and there is not much you can do about these variations. In any case, the variations are typically relatively small in the short term. While there is some variation in the rate of return you earn on cash investments, it is generally possible to protect the principal value of this asset from loss under most circumstances.

The return for cash investments is generally in line with the inflation rate, and this means that you do not earn a "real" return on cash. The real return on an investment is the return you achieve minus the inflation rate. For example, if you have an 8% return on an investment over time and the inflation rate is 4%, then your real return is 4%. If your investment return is only in line with the inflation rate (4% in this example), then your real return is zero.

It is only when you get a real return on your investment—a return in excess of the inflation rate—that your standard of living improves. If this is the case, you have more ability to purchase goods and services than inflation is taking away, and this is how you improve your standard of living over time.

Since a cash investment is a reserve asset, it should not be considered a long-term investment asset, which has return and risk that are important to manage. The risk for a cash investment is in the fluctuating interest rate, not in the principal. As you will see below, bonds generally have the opposite characteristics. How to manage your cash and invest it responsibly are described in chapter 4.

Real Estate

The second asset class mentioned above is real estate. Real estate is a very special kind of investment asset. It has the potential to increase in value over time, and, even if it does not appreciate, its value to you improves steadily as you build equity through the principal payments you make, which are built into your total mortgage payments (principal plus interest). In this book, I will focus on residential real estate, not commercial real estate, such as office buildings and warehouses.

Residential real estate is not an asset that is traded minute by minute on some kind of organized exchange with a very large number of participants, like stocks and bonds, and that has a formal quoted value at any point in time.

For residential real estate, the number of buyers and sellers is relatively small, transactions are infrequent, and each transaction is unique. There is a small fraternity of professional investors who view various kinds of real estate as assets to be traded, and they actively manage portfolios of real estate assets. This is not normally the case for individuals and their investments in real estate.

For most people, real estate is simply one of the most important assets an individual will ever have. The primary reason for most people to own real estate is to live in it. It may or may not be a great investment, but that is clearly less important than the enhanced quality of life a home provides. In parts of Texas, for example, there has been little increase in house prices in more than a decade.

Given that there has been some inflation over this period, in these areas, home ownership has produced a negative real return—that is, house price increases have not kept pace with inflation. This situation, however, does not appear to have led the homeowners in these areas to sell for what they can get and move on to something else that has more potential to appreciate and give them a real return.

The return for your residential real estate will be a function of, among other things, the demographics of the area in which it is located, interest rates, local and national economic activity, and the price you pay for it initially (if you overpay when you purchase it , the long-term return will be negatively affected, and vice versa). These are difficult aspects to quantify, but, as will be pointed out in chapter 9, assumptions have to be made about them.

Risk in residential real estate comes primarily from the way in which real estate is normally financed. Imagine the situation when your real estate is financed with a conventional mortgage. Let's say that you buy a house for $400,000, make a traditional 20% down payment, and finance the rest with a mortgage of $320,000. The difference of $80,000 is the equity in your home. Equity is defined as the amount you would expect to have if you were to sell the home and pay off the outstanding mortgage.

Now assume that house prices in your area go down by 10% for some reason and the price of your home goes down by an equal amount. You still have the mortgage outstanding of $320,000, but now the price of the house is only $360,000. Therefore, the equity in your home is now only $40,000, a decline of 50%. If the price of your home went down by 20%, which has actually happened in some parts of the country recently, your equity would be eliminated.

If you: (1) pay too much for your home and are thus vulnerable to receiving a negative real return over time, (2) borrow too much and have very little equity at the beginning, and are therefore vulnerable to losing what little equity you have if the value of your home goes down, or (3) borrow at an adjustable rate that resets upward eventually to a level that is beyond your ability to pay, you will experience the risk of real estate.

Much of this risk can be eliminated by making your purchase of a home prudently, avoiding making the three mistakes above. Furthermore, over time, real estate can appreciate in value, in which case your equity expands rapidly and provides a larger cushion to absorb any downturn in house prices or increase in interest rates. In the above example, if the value of your home goes to $500,000, your equity increases to $180,000, not counting any mortgage payments you have made.

Bonds

Bonds and stocks have quite different return and risk characteristics than cash or real estate investments, and they are the focus of the balance of this chapter. In chapter 11, I will suggest how to choose an investment portfolio using these assets that will provide the best chance of achieving your long-term objectives.

What is a bond? A bond is a commitment by the issuer, usually a government or company, to pay a fixed interest rate for a certain period of time and to pay back the initial investment in full at maturity.

For example, let's assume that you buy a thirty-year bond from the U.S. government with a fixed interest rate of 5% that pays a coupon of $50 for every $1,000 you invest. What this means is that you will receive your $1,000 investment back in thirty years, and the U.S. government will pay you $50, which represents a 5% interest payment, per year for each of the next thirty years. Unlike real estate, bonds are continuously traded in active markets on a daily basis, and the price of this bond will fluctuate inversely with the movement of interest rates.

Why does this inverse relationship exist? Why do prices go down when interest rates go up, and go up when interest rates go down? The following examples answer this question.

If interest rates for U.S. government bonds rise to 10% immediately after you buy one, for example, the $50 annual payment does not change. However, if you want to sell your bond to someone at that point, he or she will demand a 10% rate of return, because this is the return available to that person in the market for these bonds.

The price of the bond at that point will have to fall to whatever price is necessary to produce a 10% return with the $50 payment, and that price is $528.65. A bond that provides a $50 annual interest payment and a final payment of $1,000 at maturity purchased at that price will provide a return of 10%. As interest rates go up, the price of the bond must go down.

If, on the other hand, interest rates in the marketplace for bonds like this one fall immediately after you buy one to 2%, the value of the bond will have to rise to the point at which the same $50 annual interest payment and the same final payment of $1,000 at maturity will provide a 2% return. The price of the bond would rise to $1,671.89. As interest rates go down, the price of the bond must go up.

Contrast the return and risk of bonds compared to the return and risk for cash. As mentioned above, risk to principal in cash can be very small. The risk is in the interest you receive on cash, which fluctuates with short-term interest rates. In the case of bonds, the interest you receive is fixed by the nature of the bond, but the principal will fluctuate, as indicated above, with fluctuations in interest rates. In the one case, the effect of changes in interest rates is to change the income you receive, and, in the other, to change the value of your investment.

There is a relatively new kind of bond that I would like to discuss specifically at this point. It is something of which you should be generally aware, and you may want to use it in the kind of long-term asset allocation discussed in chapter 11. These bonds, which have only been issued by the U.S. government since 1997, are called Treasury Inflation-Protected Securities, and they are commonly referred to as TIPS.

Because they provide inflation protection, the coupon for TIPS, which is paid twice per year, is lower than the coupon for conventional bonds. This coupon as a percentage of the price of the bond is called the real yield. However, the principal amount of the bond is adjusted over time to reflect increases or decreases in the Consumer Price Index. As long as inflation is positive, the principal grows (it is adjusted twice per year, in May and

November) and therefore so do the coupons, which are a constant percentage of the principal. In periods of deflation, the principal cannot fall below par (the price at which the security was originally issued).

TIPS have an important tax consideration that limits how they are used. Although the positive inflation adjustment is not actually paid until the bond matures, the federal government treats the increase in the value of the bond as taxable income. What this means is that, in general, TIPS should only be used in tax-deferred accounts, such as 401(k)s, where current taxation is not an issue.

Let's assume that a TIPS of a certain maturity has a yield of 2.5%, compared to a yield of 5.0% for a conventional Treasury security with the same maturity but with no inflation protection. The difference of 2.5% is the expected level of inflation in the marketplace. It is the break-even spread between the two bonds, in that, if inflation over the period until maturity is exactly 2.5%, the return for the two bonds will be exactly the same. If inflation is higher, then the TIPS will have a higher return, and the reverse is true as well.

Basically, what the TIPS provides is a real yield that is protected from inflation. This is something that is particularly important for retirees, who are living on a fixed income. According to a portfolio manager who manages a Real Return fund, "All your objectives as a retiree are real. You want to buy a real car, lease or own a real house, and take real airplane flights to visit your grandchildren."[1]

You do not have to buy individual TIPS from the U.S. government or in the secondary market. They are also available from major mutual fund companies in the form of TIPS mutual funds.

How much of a portfolio should be invested in TIPS? This depends on a number of considerations, such as your age, your concern about inflation being significantly higher than what is priced into TIPS that you can currently buy, your investment time horizon, and the extent to which you think you have protected yourself against inflation in the projections you make about how much money you will need for retirement.

In the approach to developing a long-term investment program described in chapter 11, TIPS do not play a role until well into the post-retirement years, but at that time they would amount to 10% to 20% of the post-retirement portfolio.

Stocks

What is a stock? As will be seen in chapter 5, your financial value as an individual or a family, your personal net worth, is the difference between your assets and liabilities. The same is true for a corporation. A share of stock is a share in the net worth of the corporation. These shares are traded in formal, regulated exchanges, such as the New York Stock Exchange or NASDAQ. Ordinarily, corporations pay a dividend to shareholders out of their earnings. However, the dividend is not fixed in the way an interest payment on a bond is fixed. The amount paid is entirely at the discretion of the corporation, and it can be raised or lowered.

The return from a stock is equal to the dividend return, which is the dividend it pays divided by the stock price, plus the change in the value of a share of the corporation as determined in the marketplace. This value is determined by a myriad of factors, including how much money the corporation is making, what it is expected to make in the future, what dividends it is expected to pay, its competitive position, the level of interest rates, etc.

Today, dividend payments on average provide about a 2% return on investment for individual stocks. If the price of the stock were to increase by, say, 8% per year over a period of time, the total return for the stock would be 2% (current yield) plus 8% (price appreciation), or 10%. The starting dividend yield is known. It is the fluctuations in the component of total return related to appreciation or depreciation that creates risk for stocks.

Perceptions about the future potential for individual stocks, based on their individual outlooks, and for stocks as a whole, based on such factors as interest rates, overall economic activity, and government policies, can be extremely volatile, as will be illustrated below. Changes in these perceptions are the principal source of risk in stock investments. Further adding to the risk is that, unlike the situation with bonds, the income payment (the dividend) is not fixed, and it too can change over time. Given all the uncertainties, you would expect to find that stocks have more risk than any of the other major asset classes with which this chapter is concerned.

As I indicated in the previous chapter, compound interest is in a sense a free lunch, and it helps if you can maintain a specified compounding rate. Maintaining a specified compounding rate year in and year out is not possible for bonds and stocks. In general, the higher the assumed compounding rate, the greater the uncertainty about maintaining it in the short term. For bonds and stocks, short-term return and risk are in general positively correlated. This means that the more return you seek, the more uncertainty (risk) there is that you will get it.

The relationship between return and risk for bonds and stocks is shown in figure 2.1. This figure shows the annual compound returns for bonds and stocks for the period from 1926, which is when reliable data start, and the end of 2006, as well as a measure of the annual variability of these returns.[2]

Figure 2.1
Returns and Risks for Bonds and Stocks
1926–2006

	Compound Annual Return	One-Year Return Variability
Bonds	5.4%	-4% to +15%
Stocks	10.4%	-10% to +31%

The first thing to notice is that there is a significant difference in the compound annual returns, with stocks, with a return of 10.4%, significantly outperforming bonds, with a return of 5.4%, over the period.

However, stocks have a much more variable return pattern than bonds. The ranges of return shown for bonds and stocks are those within which the return has fallen two-thirds of the time on an annual basis over this historical period. The two-thirds range is a standard statistical measure for the distribution or spread of returns, and it is commonly used to describe the variability in returns.

For example, in two-thirds of the all the years since 1926, the annual return for bonds has been in the range of -4% to +15%, and the annual return for stocks has been in the range of -10% to +31% over the same period. As you can see, stock returns on an annual basis are significantly more variable than bond returns on an annual basis.

   This is not all the information we can get from figure 2.1. If these ranges cover eight years out of twelve (two-thirds of the time), then there are four years (or one-third) that are outside of these ranges. In fact, in two years (one-sixth of the time), the annual return for bonds was in the range of +16% to +25%, and in the other two years (also one-sixth of the time), the return for bonds was in the range of -5% to -14%. Correspondingly, in two years, the returns for stocks were in the range of +32% to +52%, and in two years, the returns for stocks were in the range of -11% to -30%.

   Even these figures do not tell the whole story. Bonds and stocks sometimes have really positive or really negative periods in sequence, and the gains and losses can mount up. For example, from the end of 1972 through June of 1974, the equity market declined by 50%. If you were invested in equities, you lost 50% of your investment in eighteen months. Periods like that are very unnerving, and, as stocks grind lower almost every day, it is easy to conclude that the declines will never end. However, they have in the past, and it is important to note that the percentage gains from these low points are usually among the best that the equity market ever produces.

   The problem, of course, is that many people become so disillusioned or so desperate that they sell all the equities they own by the time the rally begins, because it looks to them and everybody else that they will never stop going down, and so they do not participate in the rebound. You do not know what it is like to have lost 50% of your equity assets until it happens, and when it does, all you can think of is to ease the pain by getting out.

   On the other hand, those investors who, for whatever reason, are fortunate to be out of the equity market and safely in cash investments when it crashes never have the intestinal fortitude to get back in at the right time, and so they do not participate in the recovery either.

   The only investors who have a satisfactory experience holding assets like bonds and stocks are those who have a long-term horizon and who have made a long-term commitment to these assets. As a result, while they are in for the decline, they are there for the recovery as well. This is the point being made at the beginning of this chapter by Warren Buffet, one of the most successful investors of all time.

   Given the short-term volatility characteristics of bonds (considerable) and stocks (dramatic), why would anyone consider these investments? First, these are the only generic assets, other than real estate, that have the potential to give you a real return (actual return minus inflation) and thus the potential to build your real assets and purchasing power over time—they simply cannot be ignored. Building your assets over time to some level and at some rate, both of which you specify, is one of the important objectives to be discussed in the next chapter.

Second, the short-term volatility tends to be moderated as time goes by. The longer the investment period, the more likely it is that the returns and risks will look more like the data in figure 2.1. In fact, it is these data that persuade investors to make long-term commitments in the first place. Consider, as shown in figure 2.2, the returns and volatilities of those returns for all five-year periods starting with the five-year period of 1926–1930 and ending with the five-year period of 2002–2006.[3]

Figure 2.2
Rolling Five-Year Data
1930–2006

	Average Return	Five-Year Return Range
Bonds	5.5%	1% to 10%
Stocks	10.4%	2% to 19%

It is important to note that these five-year periods are overlapping—they are not discrete five-year periods. What this means is that the return for a year such as 1934, for example, will appear in five rolling five-year periods. The discrete analysis is more independent, but it is the rolling five-year environment in which we live. Unfortunately, most people are not willing to wait until they get to the end of independent five-year periods to see how they are doing.

The ranges of five-year returns shown in figure 2.2 are again based on what has happened two-thirds of the time. In the case of bonds, in two five-year periods out of three, the five-year return fell in the range of 1% to 10%. The worst five-year period for bonds, which is outside of this range, was from 1965–1969, when the total return on bonds was -2.1% per year.

Correspondingly, in the case of stocks, in two five-year periods out of three, the five-year return fell between 2% and 19%. The worst five-year period for stocks was from 1928–1932, when the total return for stocks was -12.5% per year.

Figure 2.2 shows that there is a significant reduction in the variability of returns for both bonds and stocks over five-year periods, compared to the one-year variability shown in figure 2.1. Note that the returns are actually somewhat higher, even though the variability has been reduced. This reduction in variability is a very important observation, because it suggests the importance of longer-term investment horizons.

The situation improves still further when ten-year periods are considered. Figure 2.3 shows returns by decade.[4] These are discrete, nonoverlapping periods. There is, of course, nothing special about these particular ten-year periods, but, given that people sometimes remember time in terms of decades, it may be instructive to consider returns over these periods.

The best of these periods for bonds was the 1980s, when the compound annual return was 12.6% per year, and the worst period for bonds is the return of -0.1% per year during the 1950s. The best of these decades for stocks was the 1950s, when the compound annual return was 19.4% per year, and the worst decade was the 1930s, when the return was -0.1% per year.

It is interesting to note that stocks outperformed bonds in most decades. However, in the 1930s and so far in the twenty-first century, bonds outperformed stocks

Figure 2.3
Compound Annual Returns by Decade (%)
1926–2006

Decade	Bonds	Stocks
1926–2009	5.0	19.2
1930–1939	4.9	-0.1
1940–1949	3.2	9.2
1950–1959	-0.1	19.4
1960–1969	1.4	7.8
1970–1979	5.5	5.9
1980–1989	12.6	17.5
1990–1999	8.8	18.2
2000–2006	8.6	1.1

Figure 2.4 shows returns for all overlapping ten-year periods starting in 1926.[5] The data for the decades shown in figure 2.3 are therefore included in figure 2.4. These data are similar in construction to the five-year data shown in figure 2.2, but they are for ten years, not five years, and data for all the periods are shown. I am showing data for all the ten-year periods in this case to give you a chance to look at the actual data, which are summarized for convenience in some of the figures, such as figure 2.5. Frequently, seeing how the actual data developed by period is helpful in making the summaries more useful.

Figure 2.4
Rolling Ten-Year Data
1935–2006

Period	Bonds	Stocks
1926–1935	5.0%	5.9%
1927–1936	4.9%	7.8%
1928–1937	4.1%	0.0%
1929–1938	4.6%	-0.9%
1930–1939	4.9%	-0.1%
1931–1940	5.0%	1.8%
1932–1941	5.7%	6.4%
1033–1942	4.4%	9.3%
1934–1943	4.6%	7.2%
1935–1944	3.9%	9.3%
1936–1945	4.5%	8.4%
1937–1946	3.7%	4.4%
1938–1947	3.4%	9.6%
1939–1948	3.2%	7.3%
1940–1949	3.2%	9.2%
1941–1950	2.6%	13.4%
1942–1951	2.1%	17.3%
1943–1952	1.9%	17.1%
1944–1953	2.1%	14.3%
1945–1954	2.5%	17.1%
1946–1955	1.3%	16.7%
1947–1956	0.8%	18.4%
1948–1957	1.8%	16.4%
1949–1958	0.8%	20.1%
1950–1959	-0.1%	19.4%
1951–1960	1.2%	16.2%
1952–1961	1.7%	16.4%
1953–1962	2.3%	13.4%
1954–1963	2.0%	15.9%
1955–1964	1.7%	12.8%
1956–1965	1.9%	11.1%
1957–1966	2.9%	9.2%
1958–1967	1.1%	12.8%
1959–1968	1.7%	10.0%

Figure 2.4 (cont'd)
Rolling Ten-Year Data
1935–2006

Period	Bonds	Stocks
1960–1969	1.4%	7.8%
1961–1970	1.3%	8.2%
1962–1971	2.5%	7.1%
1963–1972	2.4%	9.9%
1964–1973	2.1%	6.0%
1965–1974	2.2%	1.2%
1966–1975	3.0%	3.3%
1967–1976	4.3%	6.6%
1968–1977	5.2%	3.6%
1969–1978	5.1%	3.2%
1970–1979	5.5%	5.9%
1971–1980	3.9%	8.4%
1972–1981	2.8%	6.5%
1973–1982	5.8%	6.7%
1974–1983	5.9%	10.6%
1975–1984	7.0%	14.8%
1976–1985	9.0%	14.3%
1977–1986	9.7%	13.8%
1978–1987	9.5%	15.3%
1979–1988	10.6%	16.3%
1980–1989	12.6%	17.5%
1981–1990	13.7%	13.9%
1982–1991	15.6%	17.6%
1983–1992	12.6%	16.2%
1984–1993	14.4%	14.9%
1985–1994	11.9%	14.4%
1986–1995	11.9%	14.8%
1987–1996	9.4%	15.3%
1988–1997	11.3%	18.0%
1989–1998	11.7%	19.2%
1990–1999	8.8%	18.2%
1991–2000	10.3%	17.5%
1992–2001	8.7%	12.9%
1993–2002	9.7%	9.3%
1994–2003	8.0%	11.1%
1995–2004	9.8%	12.1%
1996–2005	7.6%	9.1%
1997–2006	7.8%	8.4%

As shown in figure 2.4, out of seventy-two ten-year periods, the ten-year return for bonds was negative in only one period—the 1950s, as indicated earlier—and it was only slightly negative. There were only two periods—the ten-year periods ended in 1938 and 1939, respectively—when the return for stocks was negative. Even in those years, the returns were not very negative.

These negative returns for bonds and stocks for a small number of ten-year periods were a very small price to pay for the opportunity to participate in the possibility of long-term returns like those shown in figure 2.1.

Figure 2.5 summarizes the data in figure 2.4, using the same format used in figure 2.2.[6] Note that the variabilities of the ten-year returns for bonds and stocks are somewhat less than those for the rolling five-year periods shown in figure 2.2.

Figure 2.5
Rolling Ten-Year Data
1935–2006

	Average Return	Ten-Year Return Range
Bonds	5.4%	2% to 9%
Stocks	11.2%	6% to 17%

There is obviously no guarantee that the future will be like the past. However, the data in figures 2.2, 2.3, 2.4, and 2.5 clearly demonstrate that historically a long-term horizon for investing in bonds and stocks provides worthwhile returns on average and that the variability of returns is reduced over what it is in shorter-term periods.

While it is critical to the achievement of your long-term financial objectives to invest in bonds and stocks, you should only invest in them with the longer-term horizons in mind. This is the critical message from Warren Buffett in the quotation at the beginning of this chapter.

One of the illusions created by the short- or long-term return volatility is that it might be possible to time one's investment in bonds and stocks to enhance returns, buying low and selling high. While this is possible for a small number of professionals who spend their entire careers developing techniques to do this and who typically manage money for large, sophisticated, institutional investors, it is not something the typical person should try.

This is another one of those intellectual distractions to which I referred in the Introduction. If you try it, instead of buying low and selling high, which is what you would be trying to do, you will probably end up buying high and selling low. The attempt will totally destroy your opportunity to use these investment assets to help you achieve your long-term objectives.

In summary, there is plenty of opportunity to take advantage of the long-term opportunities that the markets provide if you stick to a well-considered plan. However, there is plenty of opportunity to get off track, and if you allow that to happen, reading this book will have been a waste of time.

This chapter indicates that there is both significant return potential and significant risk in bond and stock investments. Given these characteristics for bonds and stocks and the necessity for bonds and stocks to be in the portfolios of most of us, as suggested above, the problem is to determine how best to use these important assets to achieve your long-term objectives. This is the subject of chapters 8–11.

Bottom Line

- Risk can be defined both as the variability of returns versus some long-term standard (relative risk) and as the possibility of loss (absolute risk).
- A cash investment is a reserve asset that provides asset preservation and a fluctuating return that is approximately equal to the inflation rate over time. It is not a long-term asset.
- Real estate investment has peculiar return and risk characteristics that relate to such important considerations as demographics, economic activity, and how the investment is financed. There is no formal market for real estate investments, as there is for bonds and stocks.
- A bond provides a stated level of income, but the value of the bond investment fluctuates inversely with interest rates.
- A stock is a share in the net worth of a corporation, and the corporation may pay a dividend on each share.
- Bonds and stocks are risky assets based on both definitions of risk indicated above.
- Volatility of returns for both bonds and stocks goes down as the holding period increases. Over all ten-year periods from 1935–2006,

for example, there have been few periods of absolute loss (absolute risk has been small), and the losses have been modest.

- There is no guarantee, however, that the future will be like the past.
- Bonds and stocks are very important investment assets, because they are the only generic assets, other than real estate, which have the potential to provide a compound return in excess of the inflation rate and thus to improve your standard of living.
- To benefit from the returns from these assets, you have to be a long-term investor and not be distracted by: (1) people or techniques that purport to be able to do better than the long-term returns these assets can provide, and (2) the short-term volatility that is a necessary and inevitable characteristic of investing in them.

PART II

Objectives

Chapter 3

Setting Personal Objectives

===

In the absence of clearly defined goals, we become strangely loyal to performing daily trivia until ultimately we become enslaved by it.

Robert Heinlein
Science Fiction Writer

===

As suggested in the quotation from Robert Heinlein, it is easy to get so caught up in the daily trivia that you think that managing it is an objective in itself. In response to the question, "How are you doing?" most people would probably answer, "I'm making progress," without defining what progress is or toward what they are progressing.

I am encouraging you to break out of this mind-set and (1) establish a formal objective-setting process, and (2) set objectives using it that are critical to your growth and well-being.

Setting objectives in the manner described in this chapter will unleash a power that you will find to be amazing—and that you will be surprised that you possess. As a result, you will accomplish much more of what you want and need to accomplish.

I do not believe that there is an alternative approach, and I do believe that you will not reach anything close to your full potential without it. You must know where you are going and whether you are on track to get there.

Introduction

In general, I think that there are two categories of people in terms of objectives: (1) those with implicit objectives, and (2) those with formal objectives that are written down, updated at least once a year, and result, in the case of a family, from a family discussion in which everyone for whom it is appropriate participates.

Setting formal objectives is the essential first step in establishing a financial management process, but it is one of the most difficult parts of the process. It is the part with which people have the least familiarity, and because of this, most people do not have formal objectives. That is, they do not fall into the second category above.

This is not surprising, because they do not know what kinds of objectives to set or how to set them. They have not considered the importance of setting objectives, or, if they have, they have not taken the time to think about them in an organized way. You can identify these people by simply asking them what their objectives are and judging their responses.

The ironic aspect of this situation is that people who have not set objectives still may have objectives. How can this be? For these people, objectives are implicit rather than explicit. By definition, people cannot operate without some sort of guiding principles—for example, wanting to give our kids a good education, wanting to be successful in our jobs, wanting to be comfortable in retirement. If this were not the case, people would not know whether the decisions they are making on a daily basis are right or wrong for them. They have to appeal to things that are unspoken and only implicitly understood, but which have not been formally addressed.

However, as you might suspect, while this informal approach of implicit objectives may generally point you in the right direction, it is not desirable to stumble along hoping to get it right. In the first place, not having thought formally about all the relevant objectives runs a risk that some important objectives may have been ignored.

In the second place, it does not allow you to set milestones or targets for your objectives, so that you will always know how you are doing. Setting objectives without having some milestones and targets that will allow you to measure how you are doing and what you are accomplishing makes the objective-setting process meaningless.

This situation is somewhat analogous to that of a person who informally sets losing weight as an objective. Somehow, he or she just never does. The good intention is just that, and it does not lead to any changes in behavior. In contrast, setting an objective for losing weight with quantifiable targets and specific dates for accomplishment empowers you to achieve your objective.

Finally, the implicit approach does not provide the opportunity to prioritize and reprioritize the objectives. Not all of the objectives you establish can be accomplished simultaneously. This means that you will have to decide which objectives are more important than others on a recurring basis. The priorities you establish may change as time goes by and circumstances change, but not having a focus at any point in time will make the objective setting process very difficult. Implicit objectives are better than nothing, but they are not nearly as good as the objectives that you formally establish with priorities and timetables.

Objectives and Categories

I believe that objectives, to be most effective, should meet the following criteria:

- There should be a small number of objectives, so that the process of achieving your objectives is manageable.
- The objectives should be written down. There is nothing like having to write something down, which is developed as a general idea, to provide the focus for a meaningful objective.
- In the case of a family, the objectives should be developed as a result of a discussion involving all the household members with the potential to contribute (starting with teenagers) and the ability to understand how they are going to be affected by what is decided.
- There must be an implementation plan for each objective with targets and milestones.
- The objectives should be prioritized.
- The objectives should be revisited at least once a year or whenever there are major life-changing events, such as births, marriages,

changes of jobs, major health problems, etc. Nothing necessarily has to change, but it is important to formally ask yourself whether any change is warranted.

I would like to emphasize the third item in the list above. Setting objectives based on family discussion, if there is a family involved, has many advantages, including the following: (1) the family is likely to develop better objectives and plans to implement them if the whole family is involved, (2) this approach has a better chance of getting necessary support (for example, if sacrifices have to be made in some way), and (3) the group interaction has the potential to improve interpersonal relationships within the family, as all the members work together to achieve their objectives.

One of the problems with beginning to think in an organized way about objectives is that the first result is likely to be that there will be more objectives than can be realistically pursued. The initial list will probably be a mix of nice-to-have things as well as need-to-have things. For example, you can establish objectives to buy a boat, take a trip, buy a bigger house, retire at 40, make a lot of money, provide a good education for your kids, save for retirement, and the list goes on and on. This is why prioritization and focus are such important parts of the objective-setting process.

The problem with having a large number of objectives is that while you have the comfort of thinking that you have covered all the bases, you have the discomfort of ending up with paralysis by objectives. This is because there are so many objectives that you cannot possibly work on all of them at once. What happens is that, after carefully listing all of them, you don't do anything about any of them, because you don't know where to start. You put the list away and forget about it.

The art of the possible in setting objectives is to set up the objectives in categories. Categorization is the first step to organizing anything. You can decide later what you want to call the categories.

The first category (Category One) consists of those objectives that have very high priority, objectives without the achievement of which the rest of the objectives become irrelevant. These are objectives that are need-to-have. The second category (Category Two) consists of medium-priority objectives, which are feasible to pursue if the Category One objectives are achieved. These are a mix of need-to-have and nice-to-have objectives. The final category (Category Three) consists of those objectives that are almost always nice-to-have, and which can be addressed when the objectives in the first two categories are achieved.

It is quite possible that over time objectives will move from one category to another, reflecting your dynamic management of your objectives. However, as suggested above, you still need to focus on a small number of objectives at any one point in time, which means that you are likely going to be able to focus at any one time only on the objectives in your current Category One.

After the initial achievement of a particular objective (e.g., establishing a cash flow management system), the focus shifts to maintaining that initial achievement. This shift is critical, because you do not want to backslide after you have made the significant personal effort involved in achieving an objective in the first place. However, this maintenance requires far less effort than the initial achievement.

To get you started on the process of setting objectives, I show in figure 3.1 examples of objectives in Category One, with implementation plans and target completion dates.

Figure 3.1
Category One Objectives

- Maintain a standard of living you consider appropriate for your income level.
  - Develop an annual budget within three months.
- Manage your cash flow efficiently.
  - Develop a cash flow management system within six months.
- Preserve your life and property.
  - Have all necessary insurance coverages in place within six months.
- Grow your personal net worth to the point at which you have enough money to live comfortably when you decide to retire.
  - Develop a plan within twelve months to achieve this level of independence.
- Achieve and maintain an environment that provides respect and support for each member of the family, if any.
  - Develop a process that allows for members to be treated fairly, provides for dispute resolution, and encourages freedom of expression within six months.
- Have fun.

-    Take time to enjoy each other, your friends, and a broad range of activities unrelated to objective setting without a timetable. There are some very serious issues involved in objective setting, but you should not overlook that "all work and no play" will, in the end, work against the achievement of these objectives.

The first objective in figure 3.1 (maintain a living standard) means that you have to develop an annual budget that includes the following: (1) all the income you expect to receive from all sources and all the expenditures by category that you plan to make, and (2) a system that allows you to monitor how you are doing versus budget in each category and make adjustments to your spending as the year develops. Living within your means in this way is the subject of chapter 6.

The second objective (efficiently manage your cash flow) addresses the fundamental issue of slippage. Slippage refers to the situation in which you are left at the end of the year not being exactly sure where your money went.

Money comes in from a variety of sources, and money goes out for a variety of purposes, and you want to make sure that there is no inadvertent slippage and waste of resources and that the whole process is set up in the most reliable, easy-to-maintain, and time-saving way. Managing your cash flow efficiently is the subject of chapter 4.

The third objective (preserve lives and property) is of critical importance, because you need to do everything reasonable and affordable to make sure that you are in and stay in good health and that there are no major catastrophes for which you are not prepared (e.g., your house burning down, losing your job, getting injured at work). Personal, property, and liability insurance are the subjects of chapter 7.

The fourth objective (increase personal net worth) concerns the steps you need to take now to give you the best chance to live comfortably by your standards in retirement and to avoid being a burden to your children. You will have to decide such questions as when you want to retire, what standard of living you want to have when you retire, and how to fund your retirement at that level. The concept of personal net worth is developed in chapter 5, and planning for retirement is discussed at length in chapters 8–11.

The fifth objective (respectful, supportive environment) is very difficult to get right, and it requires careful thought about how to achieve it. Like the other objectives in Category One, it must have a deadline for its achievement. After that, constant vigilance is required to maintain this kind of environment.

Finally, the last objective applies to life in general, whether it concerns work, home life, or other activities. It, of course, seems obvious, but not giving it the status of a Category One objective might mean that it doesn't have a priority. I am not suggesting that "fun" be scheduled, although that may be necessary, or that it isn't a good idea to have, for example, hobbies, which require a particular focus. What I am saying is that fun is in some respects serendipitous, and you should make room for that to happen.

You can see that these are very critical objectives for the maintenance and growth of you or your family, and it is hard to imagine that some of these objectives would not remain in Category One for a long time. Note that the first four objectives in Category One can be achieved by reference to the specified chapters in this book.

By listing the objectives in the way I did and putting in implementation plans and appropriate deadlines, I do not mean to suggest that these or any objectives should be considered in sequence. In sequence means that you work on one thing, and then when it is completed, you move on to the next one—one at a time. If you do that, you will have difficulty in general, and you certainly will have difficulty getting through all six in a year.

What I suggest is that you work on implementation plans for these objectives in parallel. What this means is that you start on all of them at once, recognizing that for logistical and other reasons they will proceed at different paces. This way, while you are waiting for someone to get back to you on something for one implementation plan, you can work on other implementation plans. By proceeding this way, you waste as little time on logistics and other issues outside of your control as possible and have a far better chance of meeting your deadlines.

What you consider "adequate" or how much you will need to "live comfortably" will almost certainly change as time goes by and your circumstances change. That is the reason why it is so essential to revisit your objectives at least once a year. However, just because you are unable to precisely plot out a working career of, say, thirty-five years and an almost equally long retirement period doesn't mean that you shouldn't get started based on the best assumptions you can make now.

Figure 3.2 shows examples of Category Two objectives.

Figure 3.2
Category Two Objectives

- Make sure that your children have every educational opportunity you think is necessary and appropriate, and that you can afford.
- Buy a home. If you don't have one, you will likely eventually want to have one, and the acquisition of a home requires special focus.
- Participate in the life of your community or place of worship.
- Care adequately for aging parents.

You can see that these objectives might very well be included in Category One, because they are also important. The effort here, however, is to recognize that without the achievement of the Category One objectives, the achievement of these Category Two objectives would be difficult, if not impossible. Furthermore, the Category One list is already as long as it should be.

To illustrate the differences between Categories One and Two and Category Three, I have listed some examples of Category Three objectives in figure 3.3.

Figure 3.3
Category Three Objectives

- Buy a boat or a motorcycle or an expensive new car.
- Remodel the kitchen.
- Buy a vacation home.
- Make a large donation to charity.

It is clear that these are nice-to-have objectives, but they are not nearly as important at the outset as the objectives in Category One and Category Two. However, some of these at some point might move into Category Two.

In principle, the objectives in all three categories should be unique to each person or family, developed in response to individual circumstances and preferences. However, if you think about it, the objectives I have shown in Category One are not unique. They are all appropriate for anyone, because they are the basic issues that have to be successfully addressed for you to develop an organized personal financial management process.

Given the principle mentioned earlier of minimizing the number of objectives to eliminate objective paralysis and the importance of the specific objectives listed, it would seem to be a good idea for everyone to start with the objectives listed above in Category One. It would be appropriate to move on to Category Two after: (1) real progress has been made on achieving objectives in Category One, and (2) some of the Category One objectives have been moved into maintenance mode.

Monitor your progress to the achievement of these objectives against the timetables you have set. When an objective is achieved to your satisfaction, you can either keep it in the same category or move it to a new category that contains completed objectives you are now primarily monitoring.

Please keep in mind that these are examples of objectives in the three categories. For this critical exercise to be meaningful to you, you must fill in your own objectives and timetables in each category. There is no escaping the fact that you yourself must make the investment to do this work. This is an example of the personal involvement I mentioned in the Introduction. Nobody can do this for you, and trying to get someone to do it for you will destroy the whole process.

Bottom Line

- Setting objectives is an indispensable way to unleash the power of each person.
- Setting objectives is the starting point for the development of an organized personal financial management process.
- Setting objectives should be a rigorous process involving the whole family, if any.

- Only a small number of objectives should be considered at one time.
- The objectives must meet specific criteria in order to be useful.
- The objectives should be prioritized by importance and placed into categories.
- Objectives without implementation plans and timetables have little meaning.
- The objectives should be pursued in parallel (at the same time), not in sequence (one at a time).
- The objectives should be updated at least once a year or when there are major life-changing events for the family
- Objective setting is a process that depends for its success on your personal involvement. There is no acceptable substitute.

PART III

Financial Management

Chapter 4

Creating a Cash Flow Management Process

There was a time when a fool and his money were soon parted, but now it happens to everybody.

Adlai Stevenson
Former Senator and
Presidential Candidate

Many people seem to spend an inordinate amount of time on various aspects of cash management, from keeping track of their money as it comes in from various sources to remembering to pay bills on time to avoid late payment charges, managing the actual process of paying bills, differentiating between payments that are the same every month, such as mortgage payments and those that are variable, keeping track of when bills were actually paid, and trying to get a safe but competitive return on any idle cash that may be available.

This is the condition about which Adlai Stevenson is concerned. However, it does not have to be this way. In today's world, almost all of the activities related to cash management can be organized, safely and reliably, electronically. When you have done this, you will only part with your money when and under the circumstances you choose.

It is the objective of this chapter to show you how to create a cash management process that addresses all the issues mentioned above and requires very little effort after the initial setup.

Ideally, your cash management process should operate almost automatically and in the background, and your focus should simply be on monitoring it to make sure that it is functioning properly and making key decisions about it.

Cash management is about money coming in and money going out. Let's start with money going out. The traditional way in which this happens is shown in figure 4.1.

Figure 4.1
Traditional Cash Management

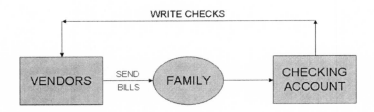

Basically, paper bills come into the family from various organizations and individuals that supply services (i.e., vendors), and then the family turns to the checking account and writes checks to the vendors. Vendors include all of those people or organizations with which you do business—governmental institutions, utilities, insurance companies, and those providing miscellaneous household support.

Many times the bills are put aside and not even opened, because there is not enough time or an easy system available to deal with them, and some are possibly even lost. This postponement leads to late charges, problems with vendors, unnecessary aggravation, and possibly a less positive credit rating than you deserve. Furthermore, this approach actually costs you money compared to the approach to be described below.

The same potential disorganization may exist in terms of income. Does your paycheck get deposited directly to your checking account? How many paper checks do you receive from other sources of income that have to be deposited by you? How quickly do you make the deposits?

There is clearly nothing fundamentally wrong with the process most families use for cash management; after all, it is the way families have been operating for decades. However, as indicated above, there is a much better and more reliable way to manage inflows and outflows that has compelling advantages. Why not take advantage of it?

There are six steps you need to take to develop the reliable, convenient, and cost-saving electronic approach to cash management that takes advantage of modern technology to make your life easier, and each of them will be discussed in detail below:

- Consolidate income deposits in your checking account
- Pay bills electronically from your checking account
- Arrange for vendors to charge (debit) your bills to your checking account
- Arrange for vendors also to charge (debit) your bills to your credit card
- Link your checking account to a money market fund
- Establish check writing for your money market fund.

Consolidate Income Deposits

The primary focus for money coming in should be on making sure that all of your income comes into one place, as opposed to having some go into a checking account, some go into a savings account, and some arrive in the form of checks that have to be deposited and can be misplaced. There are several possibilities for a central location, but the one that I think makes sense for most families is a checking account. The checking account will be the cornerstone of your modern cash management system.

To be useful as a central location and the cornerstone of your cash management system, the checking account must meet certain criteria. It must: (1) be available from a bank in your local community, (2) have Web-based, password protected, encrypted access, (3) charge no fees of any kind for electronic banking, and (4) be available with low fees and low minimum balances.

All income from whatever source should flow into the checking account, as indicated in figure 4.2. This means that your paychecks should be electronically deposited to your checking account by your employer, any dividends or interest payments should be electronically deposited by the entities paying the dividends or interest, and as many other any regular payments as possible from outside the family should be similarly deposited.

Figure 4.2
Consolidation in Checking Account

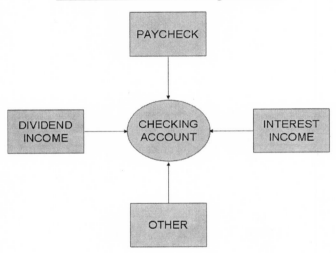

While the electronic deposits will account for the vast majority of your incoming cash flows, there will obviously be other items, such as medical reimbursements, tax refunds (unless they are deposited directly into your checking account, which would be the preferred option), etc., which will have to be deposited by mail or in person. These should, of course, be deposited as soon as they come in. This is one of the few areas in the electronic process you will develop that requires human intervention.

Pay Bills Electronically

The electronic access to your checking account allows you to set up a list of "payees," with complete addresses and your account numbers for each, which represents all of the vendors from whom you usually receive bills. This list can easily be maintained for changes in payees, changes in payee addresses, changes in account numbers, etc. When a bill comes in, you direct the institution with whom you have your checking account to make a payment in an amount and at a time you specify. The institution will either make the payment electronically, depending on the nature and technology of the vendor, or send the vendor a check in the case that electronic transfer has not been set up.

Electronic bill paying is added to figure 4.1 in figure 4.3 below.

Figure 4.3
Electronic Bill Paying

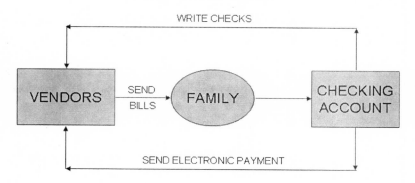

Electronic bill paying is typically free. It costs banks far less to process electronic payments for you than to process your checks (including, in some cases, sending them back to you at the end of each month after they have been cashed). The service is free to entice you to operate in a way that saves the bank money. As discussed below, it turns out that this approach also saves you money.

Among the things you can do online are: track payments to you when they come in, track payments to vendors to see when they have cleared, set up recurring payments for your regular monthly expenses, like mortgage payments, view all of your payments to a specific vendor during the year, stop payments electronically, and make transfers to other accounts you may have outside of the institution.

The object would be to never have to write a check again. This is a truly cost-effective way to operate, because writing checks costs money. The sum of the cost of a stamp, the envelopes, the checks, and your time in writing them could easily add up to considerably more than seventy-five cents per check.

If you normally write, say, twenty checks per month, or two hundred forty checks per year, the saving would be $180 per year. Clearly, you may never get to this point, because of one-time bills and other reasons that require you to write checks, but the closer you can get the better.

If you pay your bills electronically when they come in and choose the amount and the date on which you want them paid, you will not have all of the problems listed above—no lost bills, no late payment charges. This improves vendor confidence in your payment ability, and it may even lead to a better credit record.

At this point, you might be saying to yourself that taking this step makes a lot of sense in principle, but you are concerned about security and identity theft. The bank with which you will have a checking account will have elaborate and effective security measures to protect your accounts, passwords, and transactions. While nothing is ever guaranteed, the risk is very low. In fact, according to *Consumer Reports* (February 2007), "paying bills online is actually safer than sending checks through the mail."

If you stop at this step, you will have made meaningful progress. However, you can do much more.

Vendor Charge to Checking Account

Paying bills electronically is a big step toward a modern cash management system. The question at this point, however, is, why would you want to make these electronic payments if you don't have to? What if there were a way to accomplish the same objective without you having to intervene? After all, what we are trying to do is get closer to a system that operates reliably on autopilot.

The answer is to take the next step and have as many of your vendors as possible charge your bills directly to your bank account. This is a process called "direct debit."

Figure 4.3 is expanded to illustrate vendors charging to checking accounts in figure 4.4

Figure 4.4
<u>Vendor Charge to Checking Account</u>

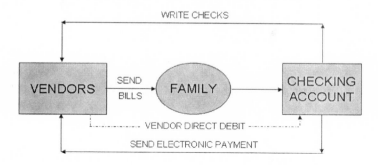

Arranging with the vendors to have them charge your bank account is very easy to do. Just try calling your electric company and tell them what you want to do. In many cases, the vendors will post their bills for you to view on a password-protected basis a number of days before the charge to your account is actually made. Therefore, you have an opportunity at that point to dispute and, if necessary, correct the bill before it is charged. If for some reason that service is not available or you do not think it is necessary to review the bill, you can still dispute it with the vendor when it shows up in your account. Vendors will typically charge your checking account at about the same time every month.

Since you have the potential to review every charge from every vendor at some point and have it corrected if necessary, there is no opportunity for a vendor to abuse the privilege of charging directly to your account. While there is some opportunity for vendors to commit fraud if you are not conducting proper surveillance of your accounts, the probability of that happening for most of the vendors with which you deal is very low.

This assumes, of course, that you allow only qualified vendors to directly debit your account. A qualified vendor is one that you feel will give you proper restitution if there is a problem. They would include utilities, local governments, etc. The local lawn service or paper delivery company would not fall into this category, and you would not want to give them access to your checking account. These nonqualified vendors should be paid electronically by you when their bills are presented by authorizing your bank to send them a check, as suggested above.

Vendor Charge to Credit Card

This step is like the previous step, with all the visibility, opportunities for dispute and correction, and convenience described above. The difference is that the vendor charge is made to a credit card and not to a bank. Given the advantages generally accrued through use of a well-selected credit card that are not offered by a bank account, such as frequent flyer miles and other benefits, this is generally the better choice. As is the case with charges to your checking account, the vendors will make the charges to your credit card at about the same time every month.

Figure 4.4 is expanded in figure 4.5 to illustrate vendor charges to credit card accounts. Note that, like other bills, the credit card bills are paid electronically.

Figure 4.5
Vendor Charge to Credit Card

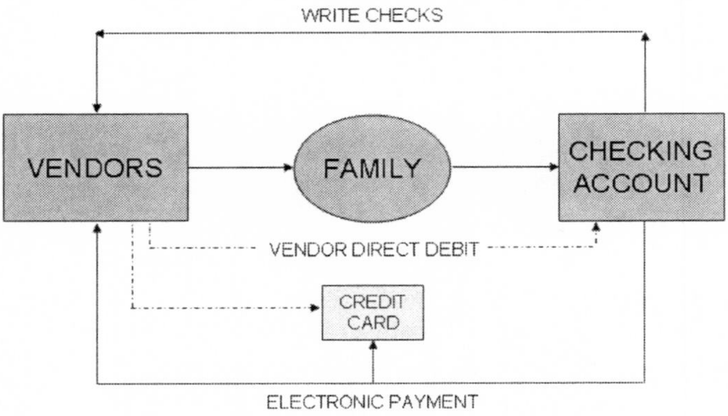

Once again, we are looking at the difference between debit and credit. When charges are made by a vendor directly to your bank account, the money is taken out of your account right away, and there are no benefits. When vendors charge your bills to a credit card, they are extending you credit, and they expect to be paid back on some basis. However, you must plan to pay off your credit card bill in full every month, or you will start amassing debt and fall victim to the "reverse compounding" discussed in chapter 1.

Link Checking Account and Money Market Fund

You have cash on hand basically for two reasons: (1) you need to have operating cash to pay your bills, and (2) you need to have reserve cash for extraordinary events. Many advisers suggest that the reserve cash should amount to six months of cash flow needs.

The operating cash should be kept in a checking account that operates as described above. The reserve cash should be invested in a money market fund (see discussion below), because the rates you earn on your cash are significantly higher. Rates on money market funds are approximately four to five times the rates for checking accounts. It is not unusual for banks to pay less than 1% on conventional checking accounts.

The problem is that the amounts in your checking account (operating funds) and money market account (reserves) are not specific, inflexible amounts, as illustrated in the examples below:

- You may have unusual demands on your checking account in a particular month, and, as a result, you will need to borrow temporarily some of your reserve cash from the money market fund. After all, this is one of the purposes of the money market fund—to back up your checking account.
- Subsequently, things get back to normal, and you want to replace the borrowed money.
- You may have a period of time when your expenses are less than expected, you are building up a surplus, and you can send some money to the money market fund temporarily or permanently.
- There may be from time-to-time some very large expenses that are too large to be paid from the checking account. In this case, there are two options: (1) transfer money from the money market fund to the checking account and then make an electronic payment from your checking account, or (2) write a check directly on the money market fund.

As you can see from these examples, there are many reasons why your checking account should be linked to your money market account. What this means is that: (1) you set up your money market account so you can transfer money directly from your checking account to the money market fund whenever you want to do so, and (2) you set up your money market fund so that it can transfer money to your checking account whenever you want to do so. With these procedures in place, you can effortlessly move money electronically between your checking account and your money market account when the need arises.

This is such a good idea that banks have started to make it possible to move funds from a checking account to a money market fund and vice versa within the same institution. This saves some time and effort compared to using a third-party money market fund, but make sure that the rate on the internal money market fund is competitive with the third-party fund.

Establishing the link between the two accounts is added to figure 4.5 in figure 4.6.

Figure 4.6
Link Checking Account to Money Market Fund

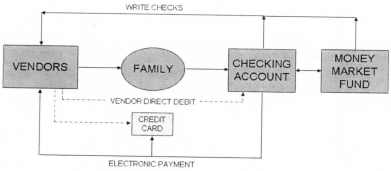

Check Writing from Money Market Fund

The final step in the process is to set up your money market fund so that you can write checks against it, just the way you would write checks on your checking account. The money market funds typically have minimum amounts for checks, such as $250, so that you don't use the money market fund like a checking account. This should not be a problem, of course, because the process you have developed does not contemplate using a money market fund in that way.

This is an important capability to have. As indicated in the fourth example above, there may be times when you would want to write a large check on your money market fund account.

Summary

What specifically has been accomplished when the six steps have been completed?

- You have minimized the number of paper bills you have to process.
- You have minimized the number of checks you have to write.
- You have minimized the time commitment you have to make to manage your cash management process.
- You have taken advantage of modern techniques to make the process as automatic as possible.
- You have focused your efforts on the really key activities, such as reviewing your checking and money market account activity to see that everything is working smoothly and deciding when to make transfers from your checking account to your money market account and vice versa.
- You have created a reliable cash management process out of what may have seemed like chaos that you can monitor and adjust when necessary to make sure that it is doing what you want it to do.
- As much as possible, this process operates on autopilot.
- You have at your fingertips a vast array of information that can be helpful in many different ways (e.g., payment history for individual vendors, the timing of payments being accepted, etc.).

Like a number of other processes presented in this book, developing your cash management system by following the six steps requires some work at the outset. I think you will be amazed at how much the advantages listed above make the effort worthwhile. Adlai Stevenson's quip may continue to apply to others, but it will no longer apply to you.

Money Market Funds

A money market mutual fund is a pool of assets, like any other mutual fund, contributed by thousands of individual and institutional investors. This pool is invested in a portfolio of short-term debt obligations (typically, money market securities with a maturities of less than one year) on behalf of the investors. These short-term obligations come due frequently, and, when they do, they are replaced by other similar obligations. When you invest in a money market fund, you buy units, or shares, of the fund at one dollar per unit.

The fund is managed by a fund management company whose objective is to earn a competitive short-term interest rate for its investors while maintaining the unit value at one dollar. All fund management companies are committed to operating their money market funds in such a way that they don't "break the buck."

There has been only one failure on the part of a money market fund to maintain its unit value at one dollar in the thirty years since the money market fund was created. However, there have been circumstances, even recently, when the company sponsoring the money market fund has been forced to put additional funds into the fund to keep its value at one dollar. According to the *Money Fund Report*, as of April 10, 2007, there were $2.4 trillion dollars invested in money market funds—an all-time high.[1]

Money market funds have provided excellent security historically. Even though money invested in them is not guaranteed by the U.S. government, as is the case with bank checking accounts (up to certain limits), money market funds can and should be used with confidence for reserve funds.

Because the funds invest in short-term debt obligations that are constantly being replaced, the interest rates they provide fluctuate with short-term rates in the marketplace. For example, during the last two years, rates on money market funds have been as low as 1% and as high as 5%. While the interest rates provided by the funds will fluctuate, the principal is secure, and this is what is necessary for a reserve account.

The principal criteria for selecting a money market fund are: risk profile, competitive interest rates over time, taxability (based on your tax bracket, it may be advantageous to use a tax-exempt money market fund, as opposed to a taxable one), and breadth of services. The funds are fairly similar with respect to the first and last criteria. The really big differences are in the rates they offer over time.

Some people think it makes sense to shop around and hop from fund to fund to get the highest rate. This is not a good strategy. There will always be some fund, but not the same fund, with the highest rate over some period—

last month, last quarter, or last year. Newspaper and magazine articles typically provide these rankings and inadvertently promote switching.

However, what matters in selecting a money market fund that will consistently earn a competitive return for you over time is its management fee (i.e., how much the fund management company charges to manage the fund).

Money market funds can target various parts of the market for short-term obligations, such as taxable, municipal, high yield, U.S. government, etc. However, all the funds operating in the same portion of the short-term market with the same charter will earn roughly the same gross interest rates. The marketplace provides the opportunity, and no one fund over time is going to earn a gross return that is very much different than the return earned by any other fund.

The gross interest rate is the interest earned at the fund level. The net interest rate is the rate paid to you after the expenses of managing the fund are deducted. The difference is the management fee. For example, assume that a money market fund, based on the sector of the market in which it operates, can earn an interest rate of 5% on an annual basis at a point in time and that its management fee is 1%. The net interest rate to investors in the fund is reduced to 4%, a 20% reduction from the 5% gross interest rate.

If, on the other hand, the management fee is only one-quarter of 1%, or 0.25%, then the net return is 4.75%. This is a reduction from the gross return of only 5%. This net return is almost 20% higher than the net return for the fund with a management fee of 1%. On a $10,000 investment, the difference amounts to $75 per year, which is money in your pocket and not in the pocket of the fund management company. It clearly makes economic sense, everything else being equal, to invest in a money market fund with a low management fee.

Credit Report and Rating

You will, of course, know where you stand in managing your cash, because you will be using the cash management system described in figure 4.6. You will know that you are paying your bills in full and on time, that bills are not getting lost or overlooked, and that you are using the types of credit you want to use.

How important is it that other people know these and other things about you? The answer is that it can be very important. For example, a recent analysis indicated that you could pay anything between $1,857 and $2,399 per month for a $300,000 thirty-year fixed rate mortgage, depending on your credit rating.[2] At $2,399, you would be paying almost 30% more for this mortgage than you would if you had an excellent credit rating and paid $1,857. Not having a good cash management system can be very costly.

In fact, there is a large variety of vendors and organizations that are interested in your credit rating. If you want to establish credit with a merchant or a credit card company, they will check your credit rating. Some kinds of employers will check your credit rating for what it might tell them about how you conduct yourself. As indicated above, mortgage lenders will price their loans to you based in part on your credit rating. Clearly, you have every incentive to maintain a high credit rating.

How do you find out what your credit rating is? There are three credit rating organizations that maintain and make available credit histories on individuals and publish a credit rating on a scale from best to worst. The three are Equifax, Experian, and Transunion. You can get your credit report and your credit rating from each of them directly for a fee at any time. However, they may have different rating scales, and they may try to sell you services you do not need.

You are allowed one free credit report each year from all three. The best way to get them all at the same time is to go to www.annualcreditreport. com, and there you can see and download your credit report from all three, based on a standard measurement scale called FICO. This is the score most commonly used by the vendors and organizations mentioned above.

Your credit report has four sections: (1) personal information about you, including your name, Social Security number, present and past addresses and phone numbers, and present and past employers, (2) your credit history, which includes the name and status of every credit card account you have ever opened, (3) public records, which include past judgments and bankruptcy proceedings, and (4) inquiries that have been made about your credit.

Given the importance of this information about your credit standing, it is essential that you make the effort to get your credit report on a regular basis (at least yearly), and verify that the information in it is correct. Is it possible that some of the information is incorrect? The National Association of State

Public Interest Research Groups surveyed two hundred people in 2004 who had reviewed their credit reports, and they found that, among other things, (1) 79% of the credit reports had mistakes of some kind, and (2) 54% had factual errors in the personal data.[3]

These are phenomenally high error rates. You are the only one who can correct them, and it is possible that some of these errors, if not corrected, could adversely affect your credit rating. You work hard to create and maintain a good credit rating, and it should not be compromised by errors you have not taken the time to correct.

To dispute an error on your credit report, contact the respective credit agency. By law, the credit agencies are obligated to respond to your request within thirty days.

Bottom Line

- Cash management is a critical part of your personal financial management process.
- The cash management process described here is straightforward to set up and will serve you well.
- Put your cash management system as much on autopilot as possible, which will free you from the minutia of operating the system and allow you to focus on monitoring your system and making the really big decisions that are involved.
- Use your checking account as the cornerstone of your cash management process.
- Pay bills electronically.
- Have your qualified vendors charge their bills to your checking account or to a credit card.
- Link your checking account to your money market fund account and set up check writing for your money market fund.
- Use a money market fund with a low management fee.
- Monitor closely your credit report and credit ratings from each of the three credit agencies and promptly correct any errors you find.

Chapter 5

Setting Up and Managing Your Personal Balance Sheet

The best and safest thing is to keep a balance in your life, acknowledge the great powers around us. If you can do that, and live that way, you are really a wise man.

Euripides
Greek Philosopher

In many ways, the balance sheet is one of your most important documents. It is basically a summary at a particular point in time—a snapshot—of your assets (what you own), your liabilities (what you owe), and your net worth. Your personal net worth is the difference between your assets and liabilities.

This is the figure on which you need to focus to determine how you are doing financially. This is the figure that would be given in answer to the question, How much are you worth? This is the figure that you will want to grow over time, the one that will determine whether one of your important objectives, the one related to providing for retirement, will be achieved. It should be monitored on a regular basis (see below).

A representative personal balance sheet is shown in figure 5.1.

Figure 5.1
Personal Balance Sheet

Assets	Liabilities and Net Worth
	Liabilities
	Net Worth
Total	

There are a number of important things you need to know about how a balance sheet is constructed. Assets are always shown on the left hand side, and liabilities and net worth are shown on the right hand side. Total assets must equal or "balance" total liabilities and net worth. That is why this presentation is referred to as a balance sheet.

The balance sheet is dynamic, in that changes in the assets or liabilities or both lead automatically to changes in net worth. For example, if assets increase by a certain amount and there is no change in the liabilities, net worth will increase by the same amount. On the other hand, if liabilities increase by a certain amount and there is no change in the assets, net worth will decline by the same amount. As will be discussed later in this chapter, the objective over time is to increase assets, decrease liabilities, and increase your personal net worth.

Figure 5.1 is a balance sheet in generic terms. However, each person needs to construct his or her own balance sheet by entering into this framework the assets they own and the liabilities they have. You will find that building your own balance sheet will require some effort and some serious thinking at the outset about things you probably have never thought about in this way before. What is an asset? What is a liability?

The types of assets that should be included in a typical balance sheet are shown in figure 5.2. There are other types of assets that you might want to include at some point, but these types will cover the vast majority of the assets you will want to include. It makes sense to include only the large categories and focus on identifying properly the assets in each one of these.

Figure 5.2
Major Personal Asset Types

- Cash
- Investments
- Personal Property
- Retirement
- Real Estate

As indicated in chapter 2, cash is a reserve asset, and it should always be invested in something. It is not money to be saved under the mattress. For most people, cash consists of money in savings accounts, bank checking accounts, money market funds, etc. Investments include any loans you have made, individual stocks and bonds, and mutual funds. These are investments in financial assets, not real assets like personal property and real estate.

Personal property includes such things as furniture, automobiles, antiques, and jewelry. It is easy to forget some of these items as you do an inventory of your personal property. Retirement investments are: (1) 401(k)s, IRAs and other tax-deferred retirement plans for which there are restrictions on accessing the assets before retirement and taxes to be paid when the money is withdrawn, (2) assets on which taxes have already been paid and which can be withdrawn only when you retire, or (3) other kinds of retirement savings plans. Finally, real estate includes your personal residence and any other real estate property you own.

The first requirement is for you to prepare a careful inventory of all of your assets and determine directly or make an estimate about how much each asset is worth. Like the cash flow and budget documents described in chapter 6, this takes considerable effort initially. However, after it is set up the first time, it is easy to maintain.

The asset side of your balance sheet, after you have collected all of the information about your assets and entered it into your personal balance sheet, might look like figure 5.3.

Figure 5.3
Personal Assets

Assets ($)	
Cash	
Checking Account	5,000
Money Market Fund	1,000
Total	6,000
Investments	
Growth Fund	10,000
Foreign Fund	2,000
Bond Fund	10,000
ABC Stock	1,000
Total	23,000
Personal Property	
Cars	20,000
Other	12,000
Total	32,000
Retirement	
Company 401(k)	24,000
Roth IRA	2,000
Total	26,000
Real Estate	
Home	350,000
TOTAL ASSETS	**437,000**

After you first complete the asset side of your personal balance sheet, you may have two reactions: (1) you are pleasantly surprised by how large your assets are, and (2) you are surprised as well by the fact that your home is such a large percentage of the total assets—in this case, 80%. For most people, a home is by far the single largest investment you will ever make.

It should be emphasized that the assets shown in figure 5.3 are not just lying around waiting to be discovered and counted. Each of these categories is there for a reason. Putting together a list of assets in these major categories helps remind you what those reasons are.

As pointed out in chapter 4, cash is a reserve asset, and you should always have enough cash to cover monthly operating expenses for a number of months. That certainly is not the case in this example. As you can see, as recommended in chapter 4, the cash in this case consists of a checking account and a money market fund.

The investments are there because having them and managing them are critical to the achievement of retirement security. There seems to be some diversification among the investments (i.e., a growth stock fund, a foreign fund, a bond fund, and one individual stock), even though, as will be discussed in chapter 10, these are not the best investments to hold.

The $20,000 for the car in personal property represents its current resale value, not the original cost. If there is more than one car, of course, this category would be larger. "Other" may be furniture and jewelry, but the total seems low based on the size and nature of the other assets.

The retirement assets consist of a 401(k) plan run by your employer and a Roth IRA. If two people are employed, the retirement plans for both of them, of course, should be included. The Roth IRA, as will be discussed later, is a relatively new kind of retirement plan. It is still restricted to withdrawals at retirement, but no tax is due on those withdrawals, because the taxes have been paid upfront.

As indicated in figure 5.3, your assets are dominated by your real estate, and this is typically the case. The home is likely to dominate your assets for some time, although the investment and retirement assets should increase significantly as a percentage of total assets as time goes by.

The value entered for the home can either be the historical cost, which is the price you paid for it plus the cost of any improvements, the appraised value, or the estimated market value.

The market value of a home is always somewhat difficult to determine, because unlike bonds and stocks, homes don't trade on organized markets every day. You, however, can make estimates of the market value by consulting with real estate agents or checking Web sites that provide comparative prices for homes in your neighborhood.

If you want to use the estimated market value approach, it makes sense to be conservative and to avoid having to make large changes in the value of the home at some point and create unnecessary fluctuations in your assets. I recommend that you adjust the home value, based on the estimated change in value, by no more than 5% to 10%. In any case, this kind of adjustment process should be undertaken no more often than once per year.

The second alternative is to pay for a formal appraisal by a certified real estate appraiser. This appraisal is generally based on actual sales of comparable homes in your neighborhood, and it is designed to approximate the current market value in the view of the appraiser.

Fluctuations in the market value of the home will, because of its dominance on the asset side of the balance sheet, create significant fluctuations in your assets. However, the values of homes do not fluctuate very much in the short term, again unlike the prices of bonds and stocks, and so paying for an expensive appraisal every year, just to value your home at estimated market value, is not really necessary.

The third alternative is historical cost. Historical cost is what you paid for your house plus the cost of improvements you have made. An improvement is a significant improvement in the nature of the house, such as adding a garage. An improvement is not painting the house or replacing your carpets. Just keep in mind that by using this value, you are almost certainly understating the value of this asset and therefore your assets as a whole.

There is no perfect answer for valuing this most important of your assets, as you can see. However, the estimated market value approach will probably turn out to be the most useful and accurate approach.

Figure 5.3 suggests that there are tradeoffs in managing your assets. For example, if you have too much money in cash, you may not have enough for your long-term investment program. If you have all of your assets in the long-term investment program, you may not be able to buy a new car and trade it in every few years. How you make these tradeoffs depends on your objectives developed as suggested in chapter 3.

The types of liabilities that are part of a typical personal balance sheet are shown in figure 5.4.

Figure 5.4
Major Personal Liability Types

- Credit Card Debt
- Installment Debt
- Personal Loans
- Home Equity Loans
- Mortgage Debt

With assets, in general you want to have as much of them as possible. With liabilities, you want to have as little of them as possible, for several reasons. Primary among them is that having liabilities means that you will be paying interest, which can compound against you as opposed to compounding for you, as discussed in chapter 1. Clearly, some debt is usually unavoidable if, for example, you want to purchase a home and are unable to pay cash, or you want to purchase an expensive car. However, managing your liabilities within limits and determining in what category you want to have the liabilities are important considerations.

Credit card debt is obviously the outstanding debt on your credit cards. As pointed out in chapter 4, this is very expensive debt, and as a result, it should be minimized. Installment debt is debt you have incurred to purchase items on credit, such as automobiles. Personal loans include money you have borrowed from friends, relatives, or a bank, the repayment of which is based on your general financial condition. Home equity loans are loans that are secured by real estate you own. Finally, mortgage debt is the debt you have incurred to purchase the real estate that you own and which you pay back through monthly mortgage payments.

Once you have collected the information about your liabilities and entered it into the liability side of your personal balance sheet, the figures might look like those shown in figure 5.5.

Figure 5.5
Personal Liabilities

Liabilities ($)

Credit Card Debt

American Express	4,000
MasterCard	1,500
Total	5,500

Installment Debt

2005 Toyota	10,000
Furniture	500
Total	10,500

Personal Loans

Loan from Parents	10,000
Loan from Bank	3,000
Total	13,000

Home Equity Loans

XYZ Bank	27,000
Total	27,000

Mortgage Debt

Home	235,000
Total	235,000

TOTAL LIABILITIES	**291,000**

Since part of personal balance sheet management is keeping a tight rein on liabilities and constantly trying to reduce them, listing all the liabilities as shown in figure 5.5 enables you to see how much they really are in total and to develop plans to address them.

For example, depending on your cash flow, which is discussed in chapter 6, you may not want to have that much credit card debt, and you will want to plan to limit your credit card debt to what you can pay off every month. There are only two credit cards listed, which is a very important step forward in credit card debt management, as discussed in chapter 6. You really should operate with only two credit cards: one that provides all the services you want and on which you charge everything you can, and one to use when, for some reason, the first credit card is not accepted or does not work.

Most of the installment debt was obviously incurred to finance the purchase of the Toyota. Otherwise, the installment debt is quite low, and this is a good thing. Installment debt can frequently be as expensive as credit card debt.

The personal loans will have to be at market rates. It is no longer possible for parents to make low- or no-interest loans to their children. However, these rates are almost certainly lower than the rates on credit card or installment debt, and, therefore, this is one of the best places to have debt, if you are going to have it. In other words, this should be one of the last sources of debt to pay off.

Home equity loans are typically taken out as an additional source of credit, and there are two advantages that attract people to this kind of debt: (1) rates are relatively low compared to credit card and installment debt, and (2) the interest on the debt is tax deductible.

The equity in your home is equal to the value of the home—in this case, $350,000—minus the mortgage loan of $235,000, or $115,000. In this case, the home equity loan of $27,000 is not large relative to the equity in the home. However, you have to ask yourself if you really want this kind of credit. These loans are frequently used simply because there is more spending than income, and they are an easy way to fill the gap.

However, the larger the home equity loan, everything else being equal, the smaller the equity cushion in case real estate prices actually decline at some point. Using these assumptions, your net equity in your home is only $88,000, which you calculate by subtracting your home equity loan of $27,000 from your gross home equity of $115,000. A decline of 10% in the value of your home (or $35,000) would reduce your net equity by $35,000 divided by $88,000, or almost 40%.

Putting the assets from figure 5.3 together with the liabilities from figure 5.5 allows you to create your personal balance sheet, with the "balancing" item being your personal net worth. This is because, as stated earlier, the total assets must equal the total liabilities and personal net worth. To put it more directly, personal net worth must equal total assets minus total liabilities.

Figure 5.6
Personal Balance Sheet

Assets ($)		Liabilities ($)	
Cash		**Credit Card Debt**	
Bank Account	5,000	American Express	4,000
Saving Account	1,000	MasterCard	1,500
Total	6,000	Total	5,500
Investments		**Installment Debt**	
Growth Fund	10,000	2005 Toyota	10,000
Foreign Fund	2,000	Furniture	500
Bond Fund	10,000	Total	10,500
ABC Stock	1,000	**Personal Loans**	
Total	23,000	Loan from Parents	10,000
Personal Property		Loan from Bank	3,000
Cars	20,000	Total	13,000
Other	12,000	**Home Equity Loans**	
Total	32,000	XYZ Bank	27,000
Retirement		Total	27,000
Company 401(k)	24,000	**Mortgage Debt**	
Roth IRA	2,000	Home	235,000
Total	26,000	Total	235,000
Real Estate			
Home	350,000	Total Liabilities	291,000
		PERSONAL NET WORTH	**146,000**
TOTAL ASSETS	**437,000**	**TOTAL LIABILITIES AND NET WORTH**	**437,000**

As I indicated at the beginning of this chapter, the personal balance sheet is one of the most important family documents. Why?

- It allows you to determine the most important figure all, which is the personal net worth (PNW). This figure is highlighted in figure 5.6, and it is $146,000 based on these assumptions.
- The PNW is important, because it is the amount you will want to grow over time at a rate faster than the rate of inflation if you are going to improve your standard of living and build a financial base for retirement. If, for example, this figure only grew with inflation, the purchasing value of the PNW would not change, and there would no improvement in the standard of living.
- As indicated above, the equity in your home is $115,000. This means that the vast majority of your PNW of $146,000, about 80%, is in the home. It also means that there is only a small positive difference between assets and liabilities when you subtract all the other liabilities from all the other assets (PNW of $146,000 minus equity in the home of $115,000 equals only $31,000). This is not a desirable situation, and one of your objectives in managing your personal balance sheet should be to increase the non–real estate assets relative to the non-mortgage liabilities dramatically over time. Otherwise, you are relying only on the real estate to build PNW over time, and for most people, that will not be enough.
- Constructing a balance sheet on a regular basis allows you to determine how your PNW is changing over time and to make a judgment about whether you are on track to achieve one of your core objectives—living comfortably in retirement.
- It gives you a framework for determining how various changes in assets or liabilities will affect the PNW. You can see how leveraged the PNW is in that small changes in assets or liabilities can create much bigger changes in PNW. For example, if the value of your home goes up by 10%, or $35,000, your PNW will also go up by $35,000. However, this represents almost a 30% increase in PNW. If, on the other hand, through your mortgage payments, you reduce your mortgage by just 10%, or $23,500, your PNW will increase by a total of $23,500, or about 16%. In fact, just eliminating your mortgage over time by itself will increase your PNW to $381,000, an increase of $235,000, or about 160%.
- It allows you to see as time goes by how to make changes in either assets or liabilities that would strengthen your balance sheet. For example, should you use some of the cash to pay off the credit card debt? Should you pay off the installment debt before you pay off the home equity loan?

- It also helps you determine what the impact is of changes you might want to consider as time goes by, such as, buying a second home or taking out another home equity loan.

You can see now why the answer to the question, "what are you worth?", is the PNW and not the amount of assets. Why is this? Consider two alternatives. On the one hand, you could have a situation in which a person had a large amount of assets and a very small PNW, because the liabilities were almost as large as the assets. This would probably be an example of a person living beyond his or her means. In this case, the answer to the question would be, "not very much", even though the assets were quite large.

On the other hand, you could have a situation in which the assets were relatively small, but the PNW was relatively large because there were no liabilities. In this case, the answer would be, "a lot", even though the assets were much smaller. As you can see in either case, the level of assets did not tell you very much about what you really want to know.

The personal balance sheet should be updated at least once per year at a minimum. However, I recommend that it be updated on a quarterly basis, at least in the beginning, when some of the obvious things that need to be changed will be identified and implemented. I also think that more frequent updating of the personal balance sheet creates a higher level of interest and involvement on the part of all of the family members, in the case of a family.

As indicated earlier, it takes considerable effort and possibly several iterations to gather all the information necessary to make the personal balance sheet truly reflect your actual financial situation. Once it has been set up, the incremental effort required to keep it current is relatively small.

As indicated above, an important long term objective is to increase the PNW faster than the inflation rate. It is clear at this point that there are only three ways to do that: (1) increase assets, (2) decrease liabilities, or (3) both.

In short, the personal balance sheet tells you a tremendous amount about your financial health and how you might improve it over time. Euripides stresses balance in all things in your life. The personal balance sheet describes one of those necessary balances, and it is one of the indispensable tools for effective personal financial management.

Bottom Line

- Assets are things you own, and they can be grouped into five broad types: cash, investments, personal property, retirement, and real estate.
- Liabilities are things you owe to others, and they can also be grouped into five broad types: credit card debt, installment debt, personal loans, home equity loans, and mortgage debt.
- The personal balance sheet presents your assets on the one hand, and your liabilities and personal net worth (PNW) on the other. It allows you to see how your PNW is affected by changes in assets or liabilities and how you can make changes as time goes by to strengthen it.
- The PNW is calculated by subtracting your liabilities from your assets. Your PNW is one of the most important measures of your financial health.
- By monitoring the PNW over time, you can determine whether you are on track to increase it faster than the rate of inflation, to increase therefore your standard of living, and to achieve one of your important goals—namely, living comfortably in retirement.
- Developing the personal balance sheet requires considerable effort to identify all the assets and all the liabilities it requires. However, once the initial investment has been made, it is much easier to maintain.
- There is no shortcut for developing a personal balance sheet and no substitute for doing it. Without a personal balance sheet, you are almost guaranteed to fail to meet your objectives.

Chapter 6

Establishing and Managing a Budget

> Annual income twenty pounds, annual expenditure
> nineteen six, result happiness. Annual income twenty
> pounds, annual expenditure twenty pound ought and
> six, result misery.
>
> *Charles Dickens,* David Copperfield

Charles Dickens is right. If you spend less than you bring in, you are in control of your life and have the potential to save for retirement. On the other hand, if you spend more than you bring in, lose control, and take on what may be very expensive debt, you then spend time and effort to dig yourself out of a hole that you have created unnecessarily. Living within your means is one of the "iron laws" of personal financial management. You ignore it at your peril.

This seems like a reasonably simple idea, but is difficult for many people to actually integrate it into the fabric of the way they live their lives. It is the purpose of this chapter to show you how to: (1) establish and implement a budget setting process that is both workable and reliable, and (2) set up a monitoring process so that you will always know where you stand relative to the budget you set.

Budget Process

Your gross income from employment is broken down as follows: (1) income that is deducted by your employer for federal, state, and local income taxes, Social Security, benefit expenses, and retirement programs, such as a 401(k), and (2) your take-home income, which is what is left after these deductions. While the amount contributed to a 401(k) plan, for example, is theoretically discretionary, in that you can choose how much you want to contribute, I recommend in chapter 8 that you contribute as much as you possibly can to such a plan. Therefore, this contribution is really not discretionary, since it is not part of a budget process.

The budget process I am going to introduce in this chapter is based on take-home income, and I will assume that you are already saving as much as you can in your retirement plans.

The first step in the process is to make a list of all of the major areas in which you spend money and want to make part of your budgeting process. Examples are shown below:

- Automobile—includes operating expenses, such as gas, oil, and repairs
- Clothes—includes all of the clothes for yourself and for family members, if any
- Family—includes babysitting, summer camp, tuition
- Food—includes purchases at the grocery store and on-line
- Furniture—includes all furniture for the house
- Holidays—includes gifts for holidays or special occasions
- Housing—includes all home services (e.g., house repairs, security, pest protection) and property tax
- Insurance—includes all insurance premiums you pay directly (not out of your paycheck), such as life insurance, disability insurance, household insurance
- Medical—includes all medical expenses not reimbursed by employers
- Miscellaneous household services—utilities, newspaper delivery, yard maintenance
- Mortgage or rent
- Pay Yourself First (see below)
- Utilities—electric, gas, telephone, water
- Vacation—includes all of your expenses for any vacations

- Miscellaneous—a useful catchall category for all those expenditure items that do not fit neatly into one of the categories you have defined. These might include, for example, dining out, contributions, etc.

There is no textbook solution to defining these categories. You have to define them in ways that are useful to you, even though they may be somewhat different from those someone else might use. The important thing is to define them in such a way that they account for 100% of your expected spending. I think these categories are representative, and I will use them throughout this chapter by way of illustration. I will show below how to figuratively deposit your paycheck and any other income into accounts representing these categories.

The one category not defined above is "Pay Yourself First." What this means is that you should set up a category in which you pay yourself first. All of the other categories are concerned with payments you make to others. This category is concerned with you paying you. This is budgeted saving, and it is one of the highest priority categories of them all. Without this category, you would be spending all of your income on living expenses and not saving anything out of your take-home income.

In the discussion of the personal balance sheet in chapter 5, I pointed out the importance of personal net worth and the high priority attached to growing it over time. One of the most important ways to grow it is to add to it by saving on a regular basis out of your paycheck(s). I also pointed out in chapter 1 the importance of starting saving early and taking advantage of the magic of compound interest. This category has to be an important part of your budget from the time you set the first one up, even if you have to give up other things to fund it.

How important is paying yourself first, say, $400 per month? If, for example, you save $400 per month for thirty-five years, at the end of the thirty-five-year period you will have a total of about $720,000 at a compound interest rate of 7%. Paying yourself first is not all that you will need for your retirement, as I will show in chapter 9, and you will need to save even more on a monthly basis as time goes by and your income grows.

This amount is a large down payment on retirement security. Imagine what position you would be in when you get to retirement if you had not had the discipline to Pay Yourself First in relatively large amounts by forcing saving into your budget. Given the growing uncertainties about the availability of government programs in the future and the inadequacy of even today's government payments to provide reasonable security, it is absolutely essential that you take charge of funding your retirement yourself as much as possible.

I want to make it clear that Pay Yourself First is a part of the budget process based on take-home income. This item should not be confused with the maximum contribution to your retirement plan mentioned above, which is also a form of "pay yourself." These are two completely different forms of saving for retirement, and you will see later that both of them are critical to achieving your objective of retirement security.

To establish a budget, you start by estimating your spending in all of the categories you have decided to use and putting the numbers down in a spreadsheet or on a piece of paper next to each category. You can estimate your spending by considering, among other things, the following: what's required (mortgage, for example), what you spent last year, what you are currently spending, etc.

The assumption in this chapter is that the withholding for income taxes is sufficient, and therefore it is not necessary to create a category in your budget for taxes. If this is not the case, then a category would have to be created for income taxes payable.

An example of the first draft of the first budget you might set up in an attempt to match income and expense based on the spending categories shown above is shown in figure 6.1(A). This draft illustrates a familiar problem for first drafts. In this example, the assumption is that your annual take-home income is $48,000.

Figure 6.1
Matching Monthly Income and Expense ($)

		(A)	(B)
Auto	*	200	200
Clothes		200	100
Family		300	200
Food		700	600
Furniture		100	0
Holidays		100	0
House		200	100

Insurance	*	200	200
Medical	*	200	200
Miscellaneous			
Household	*	200	200
Mortgage	*	1,400	1,400
Pay Yourself First	*	400	400
Utilities	*	200	200
Vacation		500	100
Miscellaneous		100	100
Total		5,000	4,000
Take-Home Income		4,000	4,000
Surplus/Deficit		-1,000	0

The problem that figure 6.1(A) illustrates is there is more spending in the draft budget ($5,000 per month) than there is income ($4,000 per month). It is never a good idea to establish a budget that, at the outset, contemplates going into debt. Borrowing money from others is the only way you can get the money to cover the overspending, and this is not an acceptable long-term strategy. Therefore, something obviously needs to be done.

The first thing to do is to identify which budgeted expenses are nondiscretionary (this means they are part of the necessary support for a modern life and cannot be easily changed) and which are discretionary. In figure 6.1, the categories shown with an asterisk are those which I would consider to be nondiscretionary. Identifying the categories this way makes the problem of too much budgeted spending even worse, because there is a smaller number of categories in which adjustments can be made.

In figure 6.1(B), I have made adjustments to the amounts shown in figure 6.1(A) in the discretionary categories to make the budget fit into the available monthly take-home income, and now the budgeted expenses are equal to the available take-home income. These adjustments are shown in boxes.

These adjustments are, of course, arbitrary, and other combinations of adjustments would also create the necessary and desired result. You might consider some of these adjustments to be draconian, but that is sometimes what is required to adjust an initial budget to the reality of the available income.

As indicated above, figure 6.1 is based on the assumption of $48,000 in take-home income. What might reasonably happen to your budget as income expands? This is one of the areas in which people get into a lot of trouble, because spending is allowed to rise with income and sometimes exceed it.

Consequently, after having made the investment to create a budget process with categories of spending that work for you and a total amount of spending that matches your take-home income, it is important to stay with it as circumstances change.

Figure 6.2 illustrates possible expense budgets for monthly take-home incomes of $5,000 ($60,000 yearly) and $6,000 ($72,000 yearly), respectively, and compares these with the original expense budget for $4,000 in monthly-take home income ($48,000 yearly).

Figure 6.2
Expense Budgets at Various Take-Home Incomes ($)

		4,000	5,000	6,000
Auto	*	200	200	200
Clothes		100	100	200
Family (if any)		200	300	400
Food		600	700	800
Furniture		0	100	200
Holidays		0	200	300
House		100	200	200
Insurance	*	200	200	200
Medical	*	200	200	200
Miscellaneous				
Household		200	300	400
Mortgage	*	1,400	1,400	1,400
Pay Yourself First		400	500	600
Utilities	*	200	200	200
Vacation		100	300	500
Miscellaneous		100	100	200

Total	4,000	5,000	6,000
Take-Home Income	4,000	5,000	6,000
Surplus/Deficit	0	0	0

Once again, the adjustments that I think would be reasonable as income increases are shown in the boxes. However, this clearly is a different problem than the one involved in the reduction of budgeted expenses between the columns in figure 6.1(A) and figure 6.1(B). In this case, as income increases, there is the opportunity to increase the budgeted amounts in the discretionary categories.

With the exception of Pay Yourself First, which has now become discretionary only on the upside, the nondiscretionary category amounts from figure 6.1 do not change with income, and this creates a sort of leveraged effect. The increase in income can be spread over fewer categories. This leverage worked in reverse in moving from figure 6.1 (A) and figure 6.1(B).

Notice that one of the major beneficiaries of the increase in income is the Pay Yourself First category. The rationale is that, given the importance of saving, you should plan to use a significant amount of incremental income to put more money aside for the future and not use it to increase discretionary spending.

The best way to Pay Yourself First is to have your budgeted saving automatically removed from your checking account each time you get paid by your employer. This way you get used to not having the money and are forced to manage the other amounts in your budget. You can do this, for example, by having the organization responsible for your long-term investment program transfer the budgeted amount of saving directly from your checking account to that investment program each time you get paid.

Pay Yourself First in as large amounts as you can afford is another of the iron laws of personal financial management. Add this to the iron law of living within your means, which was mentioned at the beginning of this chapter.

In this book, I will make the arbitrary assumptions that

- your annual income is $75,000;

- your take-home income is $4,000 per month, or $48,000 per year (this corresponds to the income shown in figure 6.1 and in the first column in figure 6.2);
- you will start with saving $400 per month, or $200 per paycheck if you are paid twice per month;
- you are 30 years old when you read this book and start your investment program, although, as you will see in chapter 11, the investment program I recommend applies at any age;
- you will retire at age 65, which means that you will be saving for thirty-five years;
- you will plan for a retirement period of thirty years, which will last until age 95.

All of the projections in chapter 9 will be based on these assumptions.

These assumptions are, of course, arbitrary. It does not matter whether your income is $50,000 or $100,000, because all of the figures, including the analysis in chapter 9, are roughly proportional. What is important is the analytical framework, and this is essentially independent of income.

The $400 per month, or $4,800 on an annual basis represents 10% of your take-home income. While this may seem to be a high percentage given all the other demands you have, you will see in chapter 9 that this is the minimum you will need if you are to achieve your objective of retirement income security. Don't say that you can't save this much or you don't want to save this much before you read chapter 9 and discover how large a contribution paying yourself first must make to your retirement security.

Budget Monitoring

The best way to monitor how you are doing versus your budget is to establish a system of accounts for each of your expenditure categories. These are not actual accounts, although they function that way. This is similar to the old idea of taking your paycheck in cash, putting portions of the cash into individual drawers labeled as expenditure categories, and taking out the cash to pay bills until the cash in a drawer runs out. However, in this case, the categories are on paper or in your computer, not in drawers.

The accounts can be set up using ledger sheets, which is the way I used to do it, using an already created computer program like Quicken, or creating a simple program in Excel, which is what I do now, if you have even a limited background in the construction of spreadsheets. It does not matter which technique you use, because they all function pretty much the same way.

Each account will be used to record all the activity for a particular expenditure category. The principal credits will be budgeted deposits from your paycheck. However, any other income (e.g., dividends) would be added as well. The debits will be the actual expenditures themselves. A sample account for utilities is shown in figure 6.3.

Figure 6.3
Utilities Account ($)

Date	Action	Debit	Credit	Balance
1/31	Regular Deposit		100.00	100.00
2/10	XYZ Electric Company	55.00		45.00
2/15	Regular Deposit		100.00	145.00

First, you take the budgeted amount of, say, $100 from each paycheck ($200 per month, as specified in figure 6.1(B)) and deposit it in this paper account. Figure 6.3 illustrates a deposit of this amount on 1/31. The next thing that happens is that there is a payment to XYZ electric company of $55.00 on 2/10. Finally, the next regular budgeted deposit from your paycheck is made on 2/15. Figure 6.3 assumes that you are paid twice per month.

Whether you are over or under budget in a particular expenditure category is easily determined by looking at the balance in its account. In the case of the utilities account shown in figure 6.3, after the semimonthly regular deposit from your paycheck on 2/15, the account is in surplus by $145.00. Note that with these virtual or paper accounts it is possible to have a temporary negative balance in one account, as long as there are offsetting surpluses in other accounts.

If your budget for an expenditure account is correct, then over time you should average a balance that is close to zero. If your balances are consistently negative, then you have not budgeted enough, and you have to adjust your budget. Of course, the reverse is also true. If your balances are consistently positive, you have budgeted too much, and you have to adjust your budget.

The final step in developing the monitoring process is to: (1) add up all the balances in your accounts (both credit and debit, if any) after you have entered all of the items in your checking account, and (2) compare the sum of the balances with your checking account balance at that time. This process is illustrated in figure 6.4.

Figure 6.4
Sum of Account Balances vs. Checking Account ($) as of 2/15

Date	Account Auto	Account Food	Account Utilities	Total Account Balances	Checking Account Balance	Difference
2/15(A)	155.00	400.00	145.00	700.00	600.00	-100.00
2/15(B)	155.00	400.00	45.00	600.00	600.00	0.00

In figure 6.4 (A), the balances in three of your accounts are shown—Auto, Food, and Utilities—and add up to $700.00 on 2/15. Note that these three accounts are shown as examples. The same process applies to all the accounts in total, but there is not enough room to show them all in one place.

However, the balance in the checking account is only $600.00. What this probably means is that there are checks you have written that are not recorded in one or more of your expenditure accounts. Go back and check through your checking account for unrecorded items, if any, and put them into the proper individual account.

Let's assume that you have checked everything and that, for some reason, the total of the balances in your individual accounts is still more than your checking account balance. In this case, you have to go back and reduce the balance in one or more of your individual accounts by $100.00, because your total account balances must match your checking account balance.

I have arbitrarily reduced the balance in the utilities account by $100.00 so that the utilities account now looks like figure 6.5. Of course, there is nothing special about the utilities account; the adjustment could have been made in other accounts.

Figure 6.5
Utilities Account ($)

Date	Action	Debit	Credit	Balance
1/31	Regular Deposit		100.00	100.00
	XYZ Electric Company	55.00		45.00
2/15	Regular Deposit		100.00	145.00
	Balancing Entry	100.00		45.00

What figure 6.4 now shows is that the balance in your utility account available to pay bills is reduced to $45.00. This adjustment has been made also in the utility balance in figure 6.4(B), and you can see that the total individual account balances now meet the requirement of equaling your checking account balance.

The other possibility is just the opposite. For some reason, the sum of the individual account balances may be less than the checking account balance. This might be, for example, because of a non-paycheck deposit you forgot to record in one of your individual accounts. Another reason might be that you have written a check that has not been cleared by your bank. Therefore, you need to examine your checking account to see if there are any items that need to be recorded in the individual accounts.

This situation is illustrated in figure 6.6(C). The total account balances are $1,200, but the checking account balance is $1,300.

Figure 6.6
Sum of Account Balances vs. Checking Account ($) as of 2/15

Date	Account Pay			Total Account Balances	Checking Account Balance	Difference
	Auto	Yourself	Utilities			
2/15(C)	155	1,000	45	1,200	1,300	100
2/15(D)	155	1,100	45	1,300	1,300	0

If after you have checked everything and there is excess, unallocated money in the checking account, you should always put it into your Pay

Yourself First account. By doing this, you will enhance your saving for the future with money you did not know you had. In figure 6.6(D), as you can see, I have credited the Pay Yourself First account with the extra $100, and now the total individual account balances match the checking account balance.

It should be noted that if you adopt the suggestion I made earlier of having your Pay Yourself First money taken directly out of your checking account by the institution responsible for your investment program, you will not be making regular deposits to this account. However, the Pay Yourself First amounts are still part of the budgets illustrated in figure 6.2.

After you have made any required adjustments, as illustrated in figure 6.4(B) and figure 6.6(D), the sum of the individual account balances, which might be described as "required" balances, will equal the checking account balance, which is the condition necessary for your system to work.

All of these figures assume that you are paid twice per month and that you have set up your budget on that basis. If you are paid once per month, you should go through this process once per month, distributing your paycheck into the appropriate individual accounts based on the monthly budgeted amounts and balancing your total required balances with your checking account.

The monitoring mechanism described above allows you to do two things: (1) determine how you are doing in each individual account relative to budget for that account, and (2) make sure that your required individual account balances are always equal to what you have available to spend—namely, the amount in your checking account.

The discussion so far has been about budgeted items and expenses in the individual accounts. However, the structure allows you to deal, for example, with unexpected and unbudgeted inflows or outflows by being able to decide into which individual account to put them.

Credit Cards

If you spend more than you have budgeted in your individual accounts, you won't end up with a negative bank balance. Your bank will not allow you to have an overdraft for very long, if at all. In fact, your checks will bounce. Your bank balance will be whatever it is; the overspending typically shows up as long-term balances on your credit cards.

Remember the point about negative compound interest, which was discussed in chapter 1. Managing your affairs this way is a very bad idea, and if you do it, it is going to keep you from achieving your long-term financial goals.

There are other ways than using credit cards to cover your overspending. One of them that has become quite popular in recent years is a home equity loan. If you have enough equity in your home, banks will lend you money against that equity. Some people find this more acceptable, because the interest is tax-deductible.

In my opinion, sources of credit like home equity loans should only be used for unusual credit demands when they happen. They should not be used to cover everyday overspending, despite the tax advantages. Using credit lines this way just covers up the basic problem of overspending.

Your card can be either a debit card or a credit card. A debit card charges the cost of whatever you buy directly to your checking account. This, of course, assumes that you have enough money in your checking account to cover the cost of the purchase. A credit card extends you credit for a short period of time—such as a month—at the end of which you are expected to pay off the credit balance. It is when you don't pay off your credit balances on time that you start getting into trouble and experience the very negative impact of reverse compounding.

Credit cards are a booming business. According to *Business Week*,[1] the average U.S. consumer has four credit cards. Fifty-one percent have at least two credit cards, 14% have at least ten credit cards, and 14% use at least 50% of available credit. These figures are amazing when you consider how expensive and counterproductive credit card debt is.

My philosophy about credit and debit cards is as follows:

1. I don't understand why people would use debit cards if they have the discipline to pay off their credit cards completely when they are due. Credit cards give you the leisure to examine and dispute your charges, the opportunity to take things back before you have to pay for them, and some time to plan for your payments. You only pay for any charges when you are satisfied with them.
2. Furthermore, according to the *Wall Street Journal*, "Debit card holders legally can be held liable for unauthorized transactions if they don't report the fraud within sixty days, while credit card customers can

only be liable for the first $50 in fraudulent charges."[2] According to Jay Foley, coexecutive director of the Identity Theft Resource Center, a nonprofit group in San Diego, "When push comes to shove, you have better protections with a credit card then you will ever have with a debit card, regardless of what the banks say with their ads."[3]

3. Debit cards should only be used by families who live for the moment and want to take their purchases immediately out of their checking account before they spend it on something else.

4. You should only have two credit cards—one that you use for everything you can to maximize the benefits, if any, from the card, and another one for those situations in which, for some reason, the first one is not accepted. Ideally, these cards should be provided by different companies.

5. Remember what I said earlier in the book about focusing on what you need and not being confused by combinations of things. What you need in this case is a credit card that will extend you credit at no cost if you pay off the balance each month by the due date, not one that is going to shower you with benefits. If you can find a credit card that meets your need for credit and has other benefits, that's a plus. However, that should not be the primary reason you have a card.

Bottom Line

- Living within your means is one of the iron laws of personal financial management.
- To live within your means, you have to do two things: (1) prepare an annual budget, and (2) set up a process for monitoring how you are doing during the year relative to your budget.
- To establish a budget, you first identify all of the categories in which you spend money during the year, decide how much you want to spend or have to spend in each category, and make sure that the budgeted amounts add up to the total of the funds you have available for the year. Your budget will, of course, vary with the funds available.
- One of the most important individual accounts in your budget is Pay Yourself First, and this is how you start saving to try to achieve one of your objectives from chapter 3, which is to provide for your retirement. Pay Yourself First is another of the iron laws of personal financial management.

- The budget monitoring process involves setting up a simple accounting system based on the individual accounts you have used to set up the budget, putting budgeted amounts of money into each category account once or twice a month, depending on how often you are paid, and taking money out of each account whenever you spend something that falls into that category.

- After depositing budgeted amounts into each individual account, you add up all the account balances, compare that total with your checking account balance, and make any adjustments in the individual accounts necessary to make the total of the account balances equal the balance in the checking account.

- If you can manage your spending in the way described in this chapter, there is no need for a debit card.

- You should have only two credit cards, one each from different companies, and you should expect to pay off the balance on each of them each month.

PART IV

Insurance

Chapter 7

Protecting Yourself and Your Assets with Insurance

Insurance. An ingenious modern game of chance in which the player is permitted to enjoy the comfortable conviction that he is beating the man who keeps the table.

Ambrose Bierce
U.S. Author

I believe that insurance of any kind should be purchased primarily to provide protection against events you consider to be catastrophic, in the sense that if an event occurred against which you were not protected, your health, net worth, and very existence would be threatened. There are other reasons to purchase insurance, but they have to do with estate planning and other considerations, and I will not discuss them in this chapter.

In general, the insurance coverages you purchase should be bought by you and not sold to you. What this means is that you should know exactly what it is that you want to buy, use the Internet to check prices and confirm that the coverage is what you want, and purchase it at as reasonable a price as you can, given the high quality you want in a provider. The implication of the quotation from Ambrose Bierce is that you want to be in charge of the game.

For most coverages, which are not provided by your employer, what this means is that you will increasingly want to purchase your insurance coverages on the Internet, if possible, and not through insurance agents. There may be some exceptions in which, for some reason, you will need the services of an agent. However, in these cases, still be sure to buy only the insurance you feel you want and need.

However, if you use an agent, I would start with one who is dedicated to selling the insurance of the company he or she represents (such as State Farm or Allstate). Independent insurance agents have potential conflicts in that they are motivated not only by wanting to help you get what you want but also by their need to sell you what they get paid the most to sell. The result many times is that you do not get exactly what you want and you may pay too much for what you do get.

The principal types of insurance are personal, property, and liability. The specific insurance coverages with which I think you should be concerned and which I will discuss in this chapter are listed below within each of these types:

Personal

- Health
- Life
- Disability

Property

- House and Contents
- Auto

Overall Liability

- Umbrella

Health

Health insurance is normally provided by your employer. This is a real advantage, because trying to put together a health insurance package on your own would be very difficult and very costly. Employers can bargain with insurance companies for a broad benefit package and reasonable rates, because they can represent a large group of employees. While the package they negotiate is what they think is appropriate for most employees, it is a "one size fits all" approach, and it may be necessary to supplement the standard package in certain cases, as I will suggest below.

The principal way in which employers try to provide some flexibility is through providing different types of options. Some employers offer what are called "cafeteria plans," which allow each employee a certain number of points. These points can then be used by the employee to purchase certain benefits at the expense of others.

Other employers have a standard menu, but they offer some choice for each of the coverages they provide. Some employers have both. Sorting through all the options typically requires some investment on your part, but once you have decided what you want, most company plans are set up to allow many choices and coverages to carry over from year to year.

What coverages should you have?

- Basic health coverage for those employed and any dependents. There is a variety of coverage plans, but the two generic kinds are: (1) in-network, and (2) preferred provider.

  With an in-network plan, you are required to go to doctors in a network assembled and maintained by the insurance company providing the coverage. In this case, often you are responsible only for a modest co-payment for many services. While this may seem to be a compelling option at first, the big question has to do with whether or not the doctors to whom you normally go and want to use are in this particular network. If most of them are, then an in-network plan is a reasonable alternative.

  With a preferred provider plan, you are allowed to go to any doctor you choose, and the plan reimburses you for something like 70% to 80% of what you pay the doctor, and you pay the balance of 20% to 30% (known as coinsurance). This plan typically also allows you to go to in-network doctors, to whom all you pay is the regular in-network co-pay. It is generally more expensive, but if you have special needs that cannot be accommodated by the standard network, or if you are willing to pay for the privilege of going to doctors of your choice and not those specified by the insurance company, then this plan is an excellent choice.

Most employers also offer a drug plan, which provides prescription drugs for your family for specified co-pays. This plan is usually integrated into the overall health plan, and you do not pay extra for the drug plan.

Some companies also offer a plan that allows you to make pre-tax contributions to an account from which you can reimburse yourself for many types of out-of-pocket medical and dental expenses, including co-payment and coinsurance, such as the 20% to 30% coinsurance in the preferred provider plan indicated above. This is a very worthwhile option to consider.

- Dental and vision coverage. These coverages are usually not too expensive and are reasonably comprehensive. They are not easy to purchase on your own.

Health insurance, in general, is evolving rapidly at this point. With the advent of new and innovative insurance vehicles—namely, high deductible health plans (HDHP) with an attached health savings account (HSA)—there is a definite move by employers to put more responsibility for medical decisions into the hands of employees. In my opinion, this is analogous to what has been done by employers to try to replace defined benefit pension plans with defined contribution plans (see chapter 8).

Life Insurance

For life insurance, I am going to focus on people with families because they involve relationships with dependents, who are typically the beneficiaries of life insurance policies. If you don't have a family or other dependents, it is not clear that you need life insurance.

You should focus on life insurance for the family members who are employed and on whose incomes the family depends. After all, the primary purpose of life insurance in the context of a family trying to protect itself is to replace the income stream(s) lost when an employed family member passes away. This is clearly a catastrophic event.

There are two primary kinds of life insurance: whole life and term life.

- Whole life will cover your life as long as you keep paying premiums. It also has an investment feature, because not all of the premium goes to pay for insurance. Part of the premium is put into an investment program that has the potential to benefit you in certain ways. As a result, whole life is generally much more expensive than term life insurance.

In my opinion, there are three problems with whole life insurance. First, you may not want to have life insurance for the rest of your life. For most families, one of the primary objectives of life insurance is to provide protection until the children are old enough to support themselves. Second, with whole life insurance, you have two programs in one—a life insurance program and an investment program—instead of just the life insurance you really want.

This is an example of what I mentioned in the Introduction. If you need life insurance, buy life insurance. If you want to develop an investment program, do that, but do it independently of your insurance program. However, it is not a good idea to buy both in one package. With a combination program such as whole life, it is difficult to determine at the outset what you are buying and difficult to evaluate how you are doing as time goes by.

One of the arguments sometimes made for whole life is that the imbedded investment program creates a savings discipline—forced savings—which would not otherwise take place. Furthermore, one clear advantage of whole life compared to term insurance is that the buildup of investment value over time inside the insurance policy is tax-deferred. That is, you do not pay any current taxes on investment income or capital gains.

I hope that the readers of this book will develop an unshakable commitment to an investment program that makes sense for them, and if they do, they will not have to rely on forced saving through an insurance program.

The third problem is the loss of the assets in the investment program if you die and the insurance company pays you just the face amount of the policy, as you anticipated. The forced saving, or cash value buildup, which represents the extra premium you have paid to buy whole life insurance in the first place, is available to you only before you die. When you die, your heirs receive the insurance proceeds, but they do not receive anything more. The cash value, as far as you and your heirs are concerned, disappears.

- Term insurance, on the other hand, is pure insurance. You need insurance, and you should arrange to buy what you need and not something else. The insurance you need is insurance to cover your family during the critical period when it is most dependent on those who are working, and the insurance would help to maintain the family's living standards if something were to happen to you.

This means that you want to look for a policy that provides insurance for a specific period of time—say, twenty years—at a premium that does not change over that period. This is called "twenty-year level term." Depending on your age, twenty-five-year or even thirty-year level term insurance may make sense.

Since this insurance is designed to replace a contribution made by the mother or father or both, the amount of insurance you should buy is a function of how much of that contribution you want to replace. Financial planners tend to think in multiples of the current income being replaced, such as ten times salary. To me, this is an arbitrary metric that does not really directly address the problem you are trying to solve. The insurance amount should be chosen with the contribution to be replaced in mind.

For example, the proceeds of a $1 million policy invested at 5%, which is probably a conservative rate, would produce an income of $50,000 per year for your beneficiaries, which represents a significant amount of replacement income for most people. This amount might be enough at the outset. However, unless it grows with inflation, it will not be enough at some point in their future. Therefore, the beneficiaries should invest the proceeds in such a way that their investment income from the proceeds of the policy is inflation-protected. That is, its value increases at least as fast as inflation.

If the $50,000 is not enough and/or extraordinary circumstances develop at some point, the principal itself could be used. Of course, you could always buy more term life insurance as well.

This is a much more direct way of calculating the amount of insurance you need than some multiple of salary. In general, I recommend that you buy as much term insurance as you can afford and need and try to replace as much of the contribution of the family breadwinners as possible.

I think that it makes sense as well to take out some insurance on the primary care-giver who may not be employed outside the home. The primary care-giver's function is as important as the contribution of members of the family who are employed outside of the home, and thus the rationale for having insurance to help replace that function is the same as for those who are employed.

Because of favorable claims experience in recent years (people living longer, among other things), rates for term insurance are very low at this time. There is no reason to use an agent to buy this kind of insurance, and there are a number of Web sites (insure.com and intelliquote.com, for example) that provide both quotes and insurance company ratings.

In this way, you can buy term life insurance from very highly rated insurance companies. For example, for a 40-year-old male of average weight and height, with no history of disease in the family, a nonsmoker, and with normal blood pressure and cholesterol levels, the annual premium for a twenty-year level term policy from a top rated company is in the range of $350 to $500 per year for a $500,000 policy. For a $1 million policy for the same individual, the annual premium would be $600 to $900.

These premiums are extraordinarily low for the value of the coverages in the case of a catastrophe. Remember that the premiums are low because the odds that the catastrophe of you dying will occur are low. However, this is an illustration of exactly the kind of insurance you want to have—namely, something that will protect your family in a catastrophic situation for which you do not have to pay very much.

Most employers provide some life insurance coverage, but there are typically two problems with it: (1) it frequently provides only a small multiple of salary in coverage amount, which, using the analytical approach outlined above, is not likely to be enough, and (2) it is not portable in the sense that you cannot take it with you if and when you leave the company. You will almost always want to have your own term insurance outside the insurance provided by the company.

Many times parents are talked into buying whole life insurance for their children. The argument is that the premiums are lower than they are later, but only, of course, because you are expected to pay them for a long time. The arguments against whole life insurance for adults are the same as for children, and you should not buy this kind of insurance. The arguments for term insurance do not really apply to the case of children, and therefore you should not buy this kind of insurance for them either.

Disability Insurance

According to the Bureau of Labor Statistics, the incidence of disability is much higher than the incidence of loss of life for most employees. What this means is that you are much more likely to lose time at work for a period of time or even forever than to die at some point during your working career. Therefore, disability insurance is something on which you need to focus.

Insurance companies are aware of these odds, and they typically offer disability insurance plans that replace a portion of your income for some period of time. There are coverages for both short- and long-term disability, and you should sign up for these if they are available from your employer.

However, there are two problems with company-sponsored disability plans: (1) they may not provide as much coverage as you want—benefits are often limited to a lower replacement percentage of income than you might want, and benefits are sometimes capped at monthly amounts that are lower than you would need, and (2) they may not provide the type of coverage you want.

Disability insurance typically covers disability with respect to a very precise definition of disability, and the definition of disability is very important. It is typically based either on your own particular occupation ("own occ") or on any occupation in which you could conceivably be engaged ("any occ"). What this means if you have "own occ" is that the disability insurance plan will pay you if you cannot do your regular job. Clearly, this is the definition that makes the most sense.

"Any occ" means that the plan will pay you if you are unable to do anything, not just your job. If you cannot do your regular job but, in the view of the insurance company, you can perform some other job, even if you do not want to do it, the "any occ" policy will not cover you.

Some companies no longer offer "own occ" insurance, and they have replaced this kind of policy with an "income replacement" definition of disability. This kind of policy will pay you if you cannot do the job for which you are qualified—the same as the "own occ" policy, but the difference is that it will pay only if you are not engaged in another occupation. Under "own occ," if you are disabled, you can still work at another job. For a variety of reasons, this is a good option to have. However, with "income replacement," you will generally not be able to supplement your disability income with income from another job.

"Own occ" disability insurance can be purchased on the Internet. However, given that some of the terms and definitions are foreign to most people, this might be one of the few cases in which talking to an insurance agent who specializes in disability insurance might be helpful. It is not likely to be significantly more expensive than the "income replacement" insurance, and a policy with this definition is the one I recommend.

Make sure that any policy you purchase is non-cancelable. What this means is that the premium is locked in for the life of the contract, and the insurance cannot be canceled except for nonpayment of premiums.

According to the Bureau of Labor Statistics, less than one-third of all workers in private industry have long-term disability insurance. Recognizing this situation and the fact that the benefits provided by disability plans they provide are not always adequate, companies are making disability insurance available for workers to purchase on their own at a discount.

One of the newer policies is called "guaranteed renewable," which is cheaper than the standard non-cancelable policy but does not provide the same security. Premiums are lower, but they are not guaranteed. Premiums can go up each year.

It is important to note that benefits from disability policies provided by the company for which you work are taxable to you, because the company has paid the premiums. However, benefits for policies for which you yourself have the paid the premiums are not taxable.

House

This kind of insurance typically consists of three elements: dwelling, personal property, and personal liability. These elements are usually packaged together. While you pay individual premiums for each coverage, the insurance company will send you a bill for the total coverage you have selected.

The dwelling portion of the insurance covers your home and any extensions to your home, such as a deck or attached garage. The object of this coverage is to provide for replacement of whatever is damaged. What you are most concerned about is the catastrophe of fire or tree damage, for example, which would make your home unusable without major repairs or replacement.

This is exactly the kind of insurance you want to buy. The incidence of loss is not very great, but the loss is catastrophic. The insurance companies know this, and they price the coverage so that you are encouraged to buy what you need, and not what you do not.

What this means is that you should buy enough insurance to cover your dwelling and not ask the insurance company to pay for small claims, such as broken windows, minor water damage, etc. If you ask for payment of these small claims, which you should be prepared to pay for yourself, your premium for your dwelling insurance goes up significantly. This process of being willing to pay for small claims yourself is called self-insuring, and you do this by deciding what "deductible" you want in your coverage.

The deductible is the amount you undertake to pay yourself, and the higher the deductible, the lower your overall premium. The insurance company will pay any expenses in excess of the deductible up to the limits of the policy. Having a deductible of $1,000 per event will significantly lower your overall premium, compared, for example, to a $200 deductible, everything being equal. You just have to be willing to pay a certain amount for small claims.

Since construction costs generally go up over time, it is critical that you make sure you have a policy with your insurance company that provides guaranteed replacement value. After all, that is what you are seeking in the first place. However, if you do not have an automatic mechanism for increasing your coverage, you may find out that you inadvertently are underinsured. You cannot afford to have that happen.

If you live close to water and there is potential risk to your dwelling as a result, you should get flood insurance, which is provided by the U.S. government through insurance companies. In some cases, flood damage could be the greatest peril, and therefore it is essential to have flood insurance if it is available.

Personal property obviously consists of all of your possessions and valuables. Coverage for personal property is usually an amount that is a percentage of the coverage on your dwelling. If that does not seem to be enough, you can pay a higher premium for more coverage. If you have particular valuables, such as antiques, works of art, or jewelry, you will have to have them appraised and take out a floater policy in an amount sufficient to compensate you for the loss of these items. It would probably be the case that, by nature, they would not be able to be replaced.

Finally, liability insurance covers you for damage to people on your property. If a guest or worker is injured, and you or something in your house is responsible, this insurance will cover you up to the limit of the policy. This kind of event does not happen very often, but it is important to have significant coverage in this area to avoid being wiped out by a catastrophic claim.

This kind of insurance and the auto insurance described below can be bought in one of three ways: (1) on the Internet through companies like GEICO, (2) through agents affiliated with one company, such as State Farm or Allstate, and (3) through independent agents who are not affiliated with any one company. My preferences would be in the order shown.

It makes sense to find one insurance company that meets your needs for coverages, prices, and service. Many insurance companies provide all of the coverages mentioned in this section, and they provide significant discounts if you have multiple relationships with that company. Examples would be insuring your second home with the same company with which you insure your primary home, insuring your car with the same company that provides your home insurance, etc.

Auto

An auto insurance policy typically provides three kinds of liability coverage: collision, comprehensive, and liability. The key issues in picking a carrier are cost, claims paying process and timeliness, and overall service. You will be asked to pay a deductible for this kind of insurance, and the larger the deductible, the lower the premium. The premium is lower because, with a higher deductible, you are paying relatively more of the claim, and the insurance company, relatively less. In general, the premium you pay can be substantially less if you increase the deductible. All the coverages have limits beyond which the coverage is not available, and the higher the coverage limit, the higher the premium.

- Collision insurance covers you for damage done to your car in an accident.
- Comprehensive insurance covers you for damage to your car that does not relate to an accident. This could include fire, theft, falling objects, and vandalism, for example.
- Liability coverage usually has three elements: bodily injury, property damage, and medical expense benefits. Bodily injury coverage pays for medical expenses and lost wages for a person you injure and may help pay for any lawsuits that result from any injuries. Property damage covers damage to another person's property (such as a home) resulting from an accident. Medical expense benefits cover expenses for insured drivers and passengers in an insured vehicle and may cover your expenses incurred in an accident involving another car in which you were a passenger.
- Liability coverage is so important that many states have requirements for minimum amounts of this insurance. However, the minimums are usually not sufficient to provide adequate protection for you, and you will want to purchase more coverage.

Umbrella

Umbrella coverage is what the name implies—a level of liability coverage on top of the basic coverages you may have. In other words, it provides coverage in excess of any individual coverage up the amount of umbrella coverage you purchase.

If, for example, the liability portion of your auto insurance has a limit of, say, $300,000, this policy will cover you for any damages in excess of this amount up to the limits of the policy. In the case of a $1 million liability claim, the umbrella coverage would pay the $700,000 difference if you had a $1 million umbrella policy.

The risk the umbrella policy helps to address is the highly unusual event that has the potential to wipe out your entire personal net worth. It does not make sense to run this kind of risk, even if it is small.

This is another example in which the premium for the insurance is very low, because the risk to the insurance company is not very high. You pay a little, and you get a lot if you need it. I would highly recommend that you purchase this kind of insurance. You can usually get it from the same company that provides your homeowners and auto insurance coverages. This coverage is not generally available on a stand-alone basis from another company.

Bottom Line

- Insurance should be purchased by you as an informed buyer and not sold to you.
- In general, insurance should be considered when two conditions exist: the risk is low, but the results are catastrophic if the risk occurs.
- You can structure your insurance purchases to meet these conditions by having high deductibles, where they apply. By insuring these kinds of risks with high deductibles, you maximize the impact of your insurance spending.
- The purchase options for insurance policies in order are: Internet, company agents, and independent agents.
- There are three principal types of insurance: personal, property, and liability.
- Most of the personal insurance coverages you need are typically provided adequately by your employer, including medical, dental, and vision. However, for some of the coverages provided by your employer, such as disability and life insurance, you will want to purchase additional insurance yourself to supplement these coverages.
- Term life insurance premiums have never been lower, and term insurance should be an important building block of your life insurance coverage.
- Umbrella coverage is another important building block, because it is a very low-cost and efficient way of protecting your growing personal net worth from catastrophic events that would extend beyond the coverage limits in your basic policies.

- Try to buy all of your property and liability coverages from the same company to get multiple-product discounts.
- Make sure that your homeowner's insurance coverage is for full replacement value, and that this value is updated by the insurance company automatically.

PART V

Retirement Planning

Chapter 8

Determining How Much Income You Will Need for Retirement and Sources of That Income

===

A whole generation of Americans will retire in poverty instead of prosperity because they simply are not preparing for retirement now.

Scott Cook
Founder of Intuit,
the Provider of Quicken Products

===

This chapter will identify the basic steps you have to take to achieve one of the Category One objectives you set in chapter 3—namely, to provide enough income for a comfortable retirement.

How important is this? According to the 2006 Retirement Confidence Survey conducted by the Employee Benefit Research Institute, approximately 70% of people are very confident or somewhat confident that they will have enough money to retire in comfort.[1] However, as indicated below, this is a remarkably false sense of confidence, which probably results from simply assuming that things will take care of themselves.

The survey, released today [4/4/06], showed many Americans' retirement expectations are like a piece of Swiss cheese—full of holes. For example, many have accumulated only modest retirement savings, underestimate the share of their pre-retirement income they are likely to need in retirement, and have made no estimate of how much they will need to live comfortably once they retire.[2]

The Fidelity Research Institute, in its 2007 Retirement Index, estimates that the typical household is on track to retire with only 58% of its pre-retirement income, and this figure includes Social Security and pension income.[3] Many financial planners suggest that you will need 70% to 80% of your pre-retirement income in retirement, and there are some who make the case for 100%. A figure of 58% is well short of these requirements.

This is bad enough, but it could be worse. If you get laid off, have medical problems, or retire early for other reasons, you might end up having to take a reduction in your Social Security income and/or to use some of your 401(k) or other tax-deferred assets much earlier than you had anticipated.

The Index found that "[m]any retirees (55%) reported leaving the workforce earlier than planned. In fact, nearly one-quarter (22%) of retirees were forced to retire early because of poor health or disability. This is an important finding since the Index found that nearly two-thirds (63%) of today's workers plan to work in retirement to supplement their income."[4]

Having at least an adequate retirement income is clearly one of your most important lifetime objectives, but as Scott Cook suggests above, most people, in fact, are not really preparing for it.

In order for you to get prepared, there are three basic questions you have to address:

- What level of income will you need in retirement, and what are the sources that you can expect to provide it?
- What is the amount of assets you will need at the time you retire to provide that level of income and what are the possible sources of these assets?
- How do you establish the investment program that will give you the best chance of having what you need when you retire?

These are difficult questions, and the answers require considerable thought. However, they cannot go unaddressed and unanswered. It is the purpose of this chapter to provide you with a framework to create your own answers to the first question. Chapter 9 will provide a framework for answering the second question, and chapters 10 and 11 will address the third question. All of these chapters should be read as a group, because they, in order, answer one of the three questions outlined above.

Retirement Income

The following are the steps that have to be followed to determine what amount of income you will need in retirement to live comfortably, as you define it:

- Project your income at the time when you plan to retire.
- Determine how much of this income you will actually need in retirement.

The first step is to estimate what your salary will be when you retire. This estimate is based on your current salary, the rate of increase you expect in your salary on an annual basis during your working years, and the number of years until you retire.

Figure 8.1 can be used to answer this question.

Figure 8.1
Estimating Income at Retirement
Multiplication Factor Matrix

Expected Salary Growth Rate

Years to Retirement	2%	3%	4%	5%	6%
10	1.2	1.3	1.5	1.6	1.8
15	1.3	1.6	1.8	2.1	2.4
20	1.5	1.8	2.2	2.7	3.2
25	1.6	2.1	2.7	3.4	4.3
30	1.8	2.4	3.2	4.3	5.7
35	2.0	2.8	3.9	5.5	7.7

To estimate what your salary will be when you retire, multiply your present salary by the number in the box that corresponds to your estimates of your expected salary growth rate and years to retirement. For example, if your current salary is \$75,000, you expect your salary growth rate to be 4% per year, and you have thirty-five years to retirement, when you reach retirement your salary will have increased to \$292,500 (\$75,000 × 3.9). If your current salary is \$100,000, you expect it to grow at 6%, and you have twenty-five years to retirement, your salary at retirement will have increased to \$430,000 (\$100,000 × 4.3).

If your salary grows at a rate in excess of inflation, then your purchasing power is increasing. For example, if your salary increases at an annual rate of 6% while inflation is increasing at 3%, you are in a position to save more or purchase more. This is because the cost of the things you currently buy is going up less than your salary. While this is a very desirable result, it is difficult to achieve in the real world.

At the moderate rates of inflation we are experiencing today (and will probably continue to experience), it would be difficult for most people to achieve a salary growth rate of 6% for an extended period. Therefore, it is better to pick a salary growth rate in figure 8.1 that provides for some increase in purchasing power (that is, greater than the rate of inflation you estimate), but which is still in the realm of reasonable probability.

For this chapter, I am going to make the assumptions in the first example above—namely, starting salary of \$75,000, salary growth rate of 4%, and thirty-five years until retirement. The ending salary at the time you start retirement will therefore be estimated to be \$292,500. For reasons to be discussed subsequently, the estimate of inflation that I think is reasonable is 3% per year, and thus the 4% annual salary growth assumption represents an increase in real income (income adjusted for inflation) each year of 1%.

The second step is to estimate how much of your salary at the time you retire you think you will need to live comfortably, as you define it. In many cases, your income need in retirement, which is typically called the "replacement rate," will be somewhat less than your ending salary for several reasons: (1) you no longer have the expenses associated with your job that you had before, such as clothes, commuting costs, extra food costs, etc., and (2) you may adopt a somewhat more simple lifestyle overall, which should be less expensive. However, there are likely to be several offsets to this general rule.

There are some expenses that may go up when you retire, such as vacation expense. Now that you have the time, you may want to travel more than you did before while you are still in relatively good health, and doing so would increase your expenses. In addition, it would be reasonable to assume that your health care expenses would be higher in retirement than they were before you retired.

What replacement rate you will need in retirement is clearly another difficult estimate to make. As indicated above, financial planners typically suggest 70% to 80% of your ending salary. I suggest that you use a number at the high end of this range, given the range of uncertainties that exists, and so for this chapter I will assume that you will need 80% of your pre-retirement income. However, I will provide some figures in chapter 9 that will allow you to see the impact of other replacement rates.

Using the estimate of pre-retirement income of $292,500, determined above from figure 8.1, an 80% replacement rate would mean that you would need an annual income in retirement of $234,000 when you retire.

There is one additional consideration for your retirement income, and that is that the required retirement income, which starts out at $234,000, must be adjusted for inflation every year. If inflation is 3%, as I am assuming, then the $234,000 must go up by 3% every year. For example, the retirement income in year two must be $234,000 × 1.03, or about $241,000, and in year three it must be $241,000 × 1.03, or about $248,000. Without this inflation adjustment, your income in retirement would not be keeping up with inflation, and your real income and purchasing power would be falling.

Sources of Income

The final step to answer the first question posed at the beginning of this chapter is to identify the sources of income that could be available when you retire. They would potentially include the following:

- Defined benefit pension plan
- 401(k) and similar plans
- Social Security
- Personal net worth

Defined Benefit Pension Plan

The traditional defined benefit (DB) pension plan is typically structured as a "final pay" plan. An example of a final pay plan is the following: to determine your pension, multiply your years of service times the average of the five highest salary years times some factor, such as 2%. For most people, the five highest salary years will be the last five years before retirement. If your salary at retirement is $292,500 and your salary has been increasing at the rate of 4% per year, as I am assuming, then the last five years of salary and the average of those years would be as shown in figure 8.2.

Figure 8.2
Final Average Pay Plan

Year	Annual Salary($)
R-4	250,030
R-3	260,031
R-2	270,433
R-1	281,250
R	292,500
Average	270,849

R = Retirement Year

The average of the five highest salary years is about $270,800. Using the representative formula above, the annual pension would be equal to 35 (years) times $270,800 times .02. This equals an annual pension of about $190,000. In this example, the pension would provide about 80% of the retirement income you need at the outset ($190,000 divided by $234,000 equals 0.8, or 80%). This obviously would be an excellent start toward the retirement income you will need.

The problem, however, is that the pension plan we have been discussing is what is called a defined benefit (DB) plan, in that the benefit is defined by formula, as indicated above, and it is a contractual obligation of the company providing the plan. These kinds of plans are a dying breed because of their expense to the company and the ongoing obligation of the company to pay into the future. Existing plans are being replaced by other kinds of plans, and very few new defined benefit plans are being created.

While DB plans are beneficial to employees who retire from a company with many years of service, there is an important disadvantage. You only earn the benefit if you are vested at the company. Vested means that you have worked at the company for a specified number of years, which qualifies you for a retirement payment in the first place. If you leave the company before you are vested, you will give up your right to a pension from that company.

My assumption is that in thirty-five years, most retirees will not be covered by a DB plan, and therefore I will describe some of the alternatives that have been created, and which are increasingly being used by companies sponsoring retirement plans.

401(k) Plan

The popular plans today include the 401(k) and cash balance plans. The 401(k) plan allows you to deduct a certain amount of money from your salary each year (up to dollar limits set by law), and have that money deposited in an investment account in your name. Taxes on the amount invested are deferred until you start withdrawing it, and taxes on the returns on the invested amount are also tax-deferred until withdrawal.

A 401(k) is a defined contribution (DC) plan, in that the employee defines the amount to be contributed to the plan out of his or her paycheck. In addition, the employer frequently commits to make a matching contribution to your account, according to a specific formula, which is based on how much you contribute. "Match" means that the company will add $1 to your 401(k) for every $1 you contribute within certain limits.

Within limits set by the plan and based on the investment options the plan makes available, you determine how your 401(k) plan is invested. Sometimes, you are limited only to investment options created and managed by your employer and/or professional managers hired by your employer. Increasingly, however, plan investment options include a broad range of mutual funds.

This is a very different plan than the typical defined benefit pension plan. Not counting the match, it is your money that is being invested in a 401(k) plan, not the company's, as in a DB plan. In addition, the company has transferred the risk to you. Since you control the investments in the 401(k), you are responsible for the rate of return over time. In the DB plan, the company is responsible for the investment performance and guaranteeing the pension payment to you.

This transfer of risk and responsibility is not trivial. It means that employees have to become knowledgeable enough to make intelligent investment decisions about allocating their 401(k) assets among the available alternatives, to evaluate investment products, and to monitor the managers and their performance.

In general, I think that 401(k) plans are a significant positive for employees, but there is a significant risk that employees will make one or both of two kinds of errors in using them: (1) invest too conservatively because they are unsure what to do, in which case they will not earn from the plan assets what they reasonably could earn and need to earn, and (2) invest too aggressively, and possibly irresponsibly, which is worse, because they may actually lose money.

Finally, the assets in the 401(k) plan are portable. You can take them with you when you change jobs and roll them over into a 401(k) plan at your new company or into a Rollover IRA at a financial institution. Given the frequency with which employees change jobs today, this is a big plus. In contrast, as indicated above, in the case of the traditional DB plan, you only get the pension benefit if you are vested. If you leave the company prematurely (that is, before you are vested), you forfeit your right to any pension at all.

An example of how a 401(k) plan with a "match" component might work is as follows: (1) the company will match 100% of your contribution on the first 3% of pay that you contribute, and (2) the company will match 50% of the next 2% you contribute, up to a maximum match of 4%.

The match is a very significant component of the 401(k) plan. This is free money, and it is typically a very important addition to the money you can save on your own. I believe that participants in 401(k) plans should put as much money as possible into these plans, because: (1) putting money into the plan is an excellent way to save for retirement, since your money is compounding on a tax-deferred basis, and (2) you get as much of the free money as possible if you contribute enough on your own to receive the maximum matching contribution from the company.

Figure 8.3 shows how this plan design actually works.

Figure 8.3
401(k) Plan Illustration
of Employee Contribution
and Company Match as a
Percentage of Salary

If You Contribute	Company Will Match	Total Contribution
1.0%	1.0%	2.0%
2.0%	2.0%	4.0%
3.0%	3.0%	6.0%
4.0%	3.5%	7.5%
5.0%	4.0%	9.0%

As you can see, if you contribute 2% of your salary, the company will add a matching 2%, for a total of 4%. If you contribute 5%, then the company will add another 4%, for a total of 9%. The 4% is the maximum contribution the company will make, and you will have "maximized the match."

Defined contribution plans, primarily 401(k)s, are by far the most significant alternative to the DB plan. According to the Employee Benefit Research Institute (EBRI), the assets in defined contribution plans have exceeded those in defined benefit plans every year from 1996–2004, and the gap is growing.[5] This is not surprising. The number of DB plans has been shrinking, while the number of DC plans is growing rapidly.

According to the EBRI, in just the period from 1990–1998, the number of participants in DC plans went from 16 million to 32 million, while the number of participants in DB plans declined from 26 million to 23 million.[6] The Department of Labor's Employee Benefit Survey (2006) indicates that the participation of employees in private industry in 401(k) plans was 43% in 2006, and this is more than twice the participation rate in defined benefit plans, which was only 20% in the same year.[7]

The cash balance plan is a hybrid of the defined benefit and defined contribution plans. In this case, the employer agrees to put a certain amount of money into an account for you, and it also agrees to credit your account with interest at a certain rate. This account is portable, like the 401(k) plan. Cash balance plans are growing, but the number of cash balance plans is not growing nearly as rapidly as the number of DC plans.

There is a variety of other individual plans that have been created to provide for retirement saving, including the Roth IRA, Roth 401(k) IRA, and the deductible IRA. For the Roth IRA, you contribute after-tax dollars (there are limits based on gross income for how much, if any, you can contribute to a Roth IRA), but your withdrawals are not taxed.

The Roth 401(k) IRA functions like a Roth IRA, only it is within a 401(k) plan. The money you contribute is after-tax, but distributions are not taxed. The deductible IRA allows you to put money into a tax-deferred account, but taxes are payable on withdrawal. There are also income limits for investing in these accounts and eligibility requirements.

Whether you use a conventional 401(k) or a Roth IRA depends primarily on what you think your effective tax rate in retirement will be relative to what it is currently. If, for example, you think that your tax rate in retirement will be much lower than it is now, you might prefer the 401(k) plan. This is because your contributions are deductible from a rate that is higher currently than it will be in retirement, and your contributions and earnings are taxed at the lower rate in retirement. In short, you don't pay taxes now at a relatively high rate, and you defer taxation to your retirement years when you think the income tax rate will be lower.

If, on the other hand, you think your tax rate in retirement will be higher, then you probably want to consider the Roth IRA. This is because you are using after-tax income to fund the Roth IRA, which is taxed at a lower rate than what you will pay in retirement, and all of the appreciation in the Roth is not taxed at all at the higher rate you expect to pay in retirement. In short, you pay taxes now at a relatively low rate to avoid having to pay taxes in retirement at a higher rate.

My focus is on helping you understand how the process of retirement income planning works, rather than on which of these alternatives makes sense for you. For that purpose, I will focus on the 401(k) plan as the principal source of retirement income from employment.

There is a temptation on the part of some who have a 401(k) to take out a loan against it. At first glance, this is appealing, because you can typically borrow at a relatively low rate and you pay the interest to yourself. However, taking out a loan means that you are giving up the opportunity to have that money exposed to the long-term earning rate for which you have planned and which is higher than the loan rate you pay.

Furthermore, if you stop your contributions to pay back the loan, you lose in two ways: (1) you will not have the contribution flow into your 401(k) for the period of the loan, and (2) you will lose the company match on the money you are not contributing. Both of these will lead to a significant reduction in the amount of money on which you have been counting for retirement. While there may be medical or other emergency reasons for taking a 401(k) loan, in general, it is something you should avoid if you are serious about saving for retirement.

Beneficiaries

Many people do not know how critical it is to designate beneficiaries for all of their retirement plans. If you fail to name beneficiaries, the assets will pass to a "default" beneficiary, which is usually your estate. If you allow this to happen, your assets will be exposed to creditors, and your ultimate beneficiaries will lose significant income tax advantages.

The custodians of these plans can make beneficiary designation forms available to you on request. These designations should be integrated with your overall estate plan and ensure that your assets pass to the intended heirs. Note that, in most cases, the beneficiary designations override any provisions with respect to these plans in your will.

It is also critical to keep your beneficiary designations up-to-date. You should review them annually and whenever a major life event takes place, such as marriage, birth of a child, divorce, or death of one of your intended beneficiaries.

Social Security

Counting on Social Security payments based on the present system is problematic. Projections indicate that we as a country are not going to be able to make the Social Security payments to those currently employed which have been promised without huge and unacceptable tax increases. In the future, it is likely that the size of the promised benefit will be reduced or the age at which it is paid will be significantly extended, or both.

Unless the system is completely changed, there will probably always be some kind of Social Security payment. However, because it is very difficult to know what it would be and it will be shrinking significantly in importance anyway, it seems appropriately conservative to assume in projections for retirement income for thirty-five years from now that Social Security payments will not play a role as a source of income. If there is, in fact, any benefit, that would certainly help, but it is increasingly clear that you are going to have to rely on your own resources for retirement income.

There is some possibility that the whole Social Security system will be revamped, simply because it is not a viable system as it stands. However, it is not prudent to count on it. The principal alternative would be one in which employees would be allowed to invest a certain portion of their required contributions into a limited range of investment options.

The advantages of such a system are: (1) the investment return you would earn would be significantly higher than the implicit return on the current Social Security program, and (2) the assets in which the contributions are invested would be yours to keep and use as you want in retirement or pass on to your heirs. Obviously, in the current Social Security program, neither of these advantages is available.

Some people may consider it to be very conservative to expect little, if any, income from a defined benefit plan or Social Security. However, in making the kinds of long-term projections required over a period of thirty-five years, considering the array of alternative tax-deferred plans that may be made available, and given the myriad of risks that might affect the projections in the first place, I think it is appropriate to be conservative with respect to these two potential sources of income.

Of the four potential sources of income in retirement outlined above, there are now only two, if we exclude defined benefit plans and Social Security:

- 401(k)
- Personal net worth

How investments in these two sources of income can produce the necessary assets at retirement is the subject of chapter 9.

Bottom Line

- There are three basic issues that have to be addressed in planning for retirement income security: (1) what level of income will you need in retirement, and what are the sources that you can expect to provide it (chapter 8), (2) what is the amount of assets you will need at the time you retire to provide that level of income and what are the possible sources of these assets (chapter 9), and (3) how do you establish an investment program that will give you the best chance of having what you need when you retire (chapters 10 and 11).

- The retirement income you need is based on a projection of your current income to your retirement date, an estimate of how much of that projected income you will need in retirement, and your estimate of inflation in your retirement years.

- Potential sources of retirement income include: (1) defined benefit plan, (2) defined contribution plan—401(k), (3) Social Security, and (4) personal net worth.

- You should not count on a defined benefit plan and Social Security as sources of income in retirement.

- Therefore, the needed retirement income will have to come from the 401(k) plan and your personal net worth, including both your real estate and your accumulated Pay Yourself First investment portfolio.

- You should contribute as much as you can to your 401(k) plan and maximize the company match.

- You should avoid the temptation to borrow from your 401(k) plan.

- It is critical to designate beneficiaries for all of your tax-deferred funds, such as a 401(k), and to keep those designations up-to-date.

Chapter 9

Determining the Assets You Will Need for Retirement and Sources of Those Assets

You can be young without money but you can't be old without it.

Tennessee Williams
Playwright

There are three basic questions about retirement planning that you have to address, which were identified at the beginning of chapter 8:

- What level of income will you need in retirement, and what are the sources that you can expect to provide it?
- What is the amount of assets you will need at the time you retire to provide that level of income and what are the possible sources of these assets?
- How do you establish the investment program that will give you the best chance of having what you need when you retire?

The first question was addressed in chapter 8. The second question will be answered in this chapter. Finally, the answer to the third question is the subject of chapter 10 and chapter 11. As suggested earlier, these four chapters should be read as a whole.

Amount of Assets Needed

What did we determine in chapter 8?

- You will need an income of $234,000 at the time of retirement, which will have to increase annually at least at the rate of inflation.
- All of the tax-deferred assets will be in a 401(k) plan.
- There will be no defined benefit pension plan.
- You cannot count on Social Security to be a meaningful component of your retirement income.
- Therefore, a significant portion of retirement income will have to come from your own resources.

Estimating the rate of inflation over a long retirement period that starts, perhaps, thirty-five years in the future is obviously very difficult. However, some assumption has to be made in order to determine the required assets, and I will assume that the inflation rate is 3% in retirement, just as it is in the pre-retirement period. The importance of this assumption can be analyzed, and I will show the results below.

The required assets in millions of dollars necessary at retirement thirty-five years from now to provide an annual income of $234,000 in retirement adjusted for 3% inflation each year are shown in figure 9.1.

Figure 9.1
Required Assets ($ million) at Retirement
at Projected Inflation Rate of 3% in Retirement

Projected Asset Growth Rate in Retirement (%)

Number of Retirement Years	5	6	6.5	7	8
20	3.7	3.4	3.3	3.1	2.9
25	4.5	4.0	3.8	3.6	3.2
30	5.1	4.5	4.2	4.0	3.6
35	5.7	4.9	4.6	4.3	3.8

The required assets depend on the projected asset growth rate in retirement, the length of the retirement period, and the projected inflation rate applied to the retirement income. In figure 9.1, you can see how the required assets change as a function of the projected asset growth rate, assuming an inflation rate of 3%, and various retirement periods

For example, if you think that your assets can grow at 8% in retirement, you have twenty-five years to retirement, and the expected inflation rate is 3%, the assets you will need at retirement are about $3.2 million. As you can see, for a constant retirement period, the required assets are very sensitive to the projected asset growth rate in retirement. If the retirement period is expected to be, say, thirty-five years, the required assets at a 5% asset growth rate are $5.7 million, compared to $3.8 million at an 8% projected asset growth rate, a difference of 50%.

On the other hand, you can see in figure 9.2 how the required assets change with the assumed inflation rate, given a constant projected asset growth rate and various retirement periods:

Figure 9.2
Required Assets ($ million) at Retirement
Projected Asset Growth of 6.5% in Retirement

Projected Inflation Rate in Retirement (%)

Number of Retirement Years	1	2	3	4	5
20	2.8	3.0	3.3	3.6	3.9
25	3.1	3.4	3.8	4.2	4.7
30	3.4	3.8	4.2	4.8	5.4
35	3.6	4.1	4.6	5.3	6.1

As you can see, the required assets are also quite sensitive to the inflation rate, ranging from $3.4 million to $5.4 million for a thirty-year retirement time horizon, depending on the inflation rate, at a 6.5% projected asset growth rate. However, long-term inflation rates of 1% or 5% are unrealistic, because they are inconsistent with our country's objective of full employment at moderate inflation rates. A realistic range is 2% to 4%, and 3% is a reasonable central tendency.

While there still is considerable variability in the required assets at retirement, the range is not sufficient to alter the structure of the analysis presented in the balance of this chapter. This is also true of the possible variations of the required assets at retirement in figure 9.1.

As I will outline in chapter 10, I think that an asset growth rate of 6.5% in retirement is a reasonable assumption, and I am assuming that the retirement period stretches for thirty years until age 95. That means that you would have to have $4.2 million when you retire.

However, having an objective of total assets in excess of this amount is helpful for two reasons: (1) there is a large number of assumptions that have to be made to get to this point, and, although I think the ones I have illustrated are conservative and realistic, something might go wrong, and (2) no formal allowance has been made in the assumptions about the required income to pay for rising costs of health care as you get closer to and enter into retirement. For this reason alone, you should be projecting an asset total in excess of what you think you will need at retirement.

How significant the cost of health care can be is demonstrated by a study by the Employee Benefit Research Institute in 2006, which determined that a couple retiring then with normal life expectancy (82 for men and 85 for women) would need $295,000 to cover premiums for health insurance and out-of-pocket expenses in retirement.[1]

If a couple retires thirty-five years from now and health care costs rise by only 6% per year, they would need more than $2 million for the same coverage at that time. It is very difficult to imagine how assets of this amount could be accumulated on top of the $4.2 million you have already calculated that you will need for retirement.

The required assets of $4.2 million in figure 9.1 are calculated so that: (1) they will pay all the required payments for thirty years in retirement, adjusted for inflation of 3%, and (2) they will be liquidated by the end of the thirtieth year. You will live off of and ultimately exhaust this amount of assets, depending on the assumptions, with nothing left for you or posterity. Obviously, you will have to reach retirement with more than $4.2 million in assets to have any assets to leave to your heirs.

Sources of Assets

What are the sources of assets that could produce a portfolio this large? As outlined in chapter 8, the only possibilities are

- the tax-deferred assets, which we are assuming are represented by the 401(k). Remember that taxes are ultimately payable on these assets and any income related to them, as will be discussed below;
- Personal net worth—this is the non–tax-deferred amount you have accumulated, principally Pay Yourself First assets and the value of your home.

401(k)

Let's look at the tax-deferred assets first. If your current salary is $75,000, you contribute 4% of your salary to your 401(k) plan, your employer contributes another 4% in its match (so that you start with an investment of $6,000 per year), your salary grows at 4%, and the 401(k) assets earn a rate of return of 7% over a working life of thirty-five years, the value of your portfolio at the end of thirty-five years would be $1.43 million, as shown in figure 9.3. The projected asset growth rate of 7% in the pre-retirement period I will also develop in the next chapter.

Figure 9.3
Available Assets at Retirement in Thirty-five Years ($)

Projected Asset Growth Rate Pre-Retirement (%)

		5	6	7	8	9
Employee	6	740,000	890,000	1,070,000	1,310,000	1,600,000
Plus	7	860,000	1,040,000	1,250,000	1,530,000	1,870,000
Employer	8	990,000	1,180,000	1,430,000	1,740,000	2,130,000
Contribution	9	1,110,000	1,330,000	1,610,000	1,960,000	2,400,000
(%)	10	1,230,000	1,480,000	1,790,000	2,180,000	2,670,000

The available assets at retirement based on other combinations of: (1) the sum of your contribution and company match, and (2) the rate of return earned on the portfolio are also shown in figure 9.3.

The discussion about what the accumulated 401(k) assets might be in thirty-five years assumes that funding starts at age 30. However, according to the EBRI, the median (or midpoint, with half above and half below) amount invested in a 401(k) plan was $102,000 in 1999.[2] That figure applies to participants of all ages. It is reasonable to assume that there are already some tax-deferred assets by age 30. If we assume that amount is, say, $50,000, then using the same assumed rate of return of 7% used above, this amount would grow to about $530,000 in thirty-five years.

Based on these assumptions, the total amount of tax-deferred assets at retirement would be $1,430,000 plus $530,000, or $1.96 million.

The tax-deferred assets make a very important contribution to the necessary total assets of $4.2 million, but they are obviously not enough. Now let's look at the personal net worth, starting with your house.

Real Estate

In chapter 5, your house was valued at $350,000. What will this house be worth at retirement?

It is reasonable to assume that there will be some improvement over the next thirty-five years in the value of this investment, but, of course, it is very difficult to estimate how fast the value will appreciate. I will assume that real estate values in your area will appreciate at a rate slightly in excess of the inflation rate of 3% we have been assuming, or 4%. Based on this assumption, the value of your house thirty-five years from now will have increased to about $1.4 million. It, of course, does not have to be the same house. This amount applies to whatever real estate you own at retirement.

The mortgage you assumed when you bought your house originally will have been paid off by this time through your monthly cash flow, and so the value of your home does not have to be reduced by any debt outstanding. This, of course, assumes that you have not taken out a home equity loan in the interim.

Pay Yourself First

The final component of the assets you have available at retirement consists of assets you have accumulated yourself during your working years.

Since the value of your retirement assets and house together will amount to $3.36 million ($1,960,000 + $1,400,000), based on the amounts developed above, and since you will need significantly more than that to provide the income in retirement that was determined above, you can see the importance of your personal saving.

This is why it is so important to pay yourself first, as suggested in chapter 6. If you don't do this and do it early, your standard of living in retirement may be significantly reduced.

In chapter 6, the amount specified for saving at an income of $75,000 and a take-home income of $48,000 ($4,000 per month) is $200 per paycheck, or $4,800 per year. If you were able to save this much per paycheck and you are paid twice per month, the value of your accumulated saving in thirty-five years at a compound annual return of 7% would be about $720,000.

Based on the same assumptions, if you could add $200 more per paycheck (so that you are now saving $400 per paycheck or $9,600 per year) to your savings at the end of ten years, at retirement at the end of twenty-five years you would have an additional $330,000.

Finally, if at the end of twenty years you could add another $200 per paycheck to your savings (now you are up to $600 per paycheck or $14,400 per year), you would have an additional $130,000 at retirement fifteen years later. Thus, the total assets available from Pay Yourself First at retirement would be $1.18 million ($720,000 + $330,000 + $130,000).

We have assumed that you contribute 4% of your salary ($75,000) to your 401(k), which is $3,000 per year at the outset. We have also assumed that you start your Pay Yourself First program with $200 per paycheck, if you are paid twice per month, which is $4,800. The total of your tax-deferred and after-tax saving is thus $7,800. This represents a little more than 10% of your gross income of $75,000, and it would be considered by many financial planning experts as a very high percentage.

In fact, as your salary grows over time at the 4% rate specified in chapter 8, your commitment to saving will stay at this high level. For example, at the end of twenty years, your salary would be about $165,000. At that time, we are assuming that you start saving $14,400 per year in your Pay Yourself First program. You are still putting 4% of your salary into your 401(k), which would be $6,600.

The total saving would be $14,400 + $6,600, or $21,000. At that point, your total saving would represent $21,000 / $165,000, or about 13% of your income. However, this would be the peak saving rate during your working career, because from here on your income will be growing faster than the amount you are saving As your income grows from this point for the next fifteen years to $292,500, the total saving per year grows to about $26,000. Therefore, the saving rate when you retire will be $26,000 / $292,500, or about 9%.

These savings rates may seem high. However, remember that the purpose of the saving is to create as large a savings pool as you can as early as you can to take advantage of the magic of compound interest. As you will see below, the accumulated savings from your 401(k) and your Pay Yourself First portfolio are key elements in the accumulation of the assets needed at retirement.

Total Assets

The total assets projected to be available at retirement would then be as shown in figure 9.4.

Figure 9.4
Total Assets Available
at Retirement ($)

Tax-Deferred	1,960,000
Real Estate	1,400,000
Pay Yourself	
-$200 per Paycheck for Thirty-five Years	720,000
-$200 More per Paycheck for Twenty-five Years	330,000
-$200 per Paycheck More for Fifteen Years	130,000
	1,180,000
TOTAL	4,540,000

The total assets from these three sources add up to over $4.5 million, which is in excess of the asset total of $4.2 million that is needed to provide an annual income in retirement of $234,000, adjusted for inflation, as determined above.

You can see in figure 9.4 how important each of the investment components (not including the real estate) you control is and what the total would be like without either of them at the specified levels of investment. The important point is that, unless you want to fall well short of your objective for income in retirement, you have to make the sacrifices necessary to achieve the specified levels of investment for each of them.

Note in particular the critical importance of Pay Yourself First in the overall picture. Pay Yourself First is the smallest potential asset category, and it amounts to about 25% of the total. However, without it, you would be able to sustain an income level in retirement that is only about three-fourths of what you say you will need.

The total for Pay Yourself First is the ultimate proof of several important concepts we have discussed in this book: (1) start early, (2) save as much as you can, and (3) take advantage of the magic of compound interest, as discussed in chapter 1, to reach your retirement objective.

The quote from Tennessee Williams at the beginning of the chapter captures the essence of what I have been saying throughout this book. You can afford to be without some money for current consumption while you are young and saving for retirement. It is likely that you will end up "old without [money]" if you don't take advantage of the opportunity you have when you are young to put as much as you can afford into your 401(k) and Pay Yourself First accounts.

Special Considerations

Real Estate

The assumption in figure 9.4 is that the real estate investment is available to help fund your retirement. However, you will still need a place to live in retirement, and consequently not all of the value of your house may be available to you to fund your retirement.

One reasonable assumption to make is that you will sell your house and move into a smaller house when you retire. Let's assume that the new house will cost you 70% of the value of your current house at retirement, or $980,000. If this is the case, then you will be able to free up $420,000

($1,400,000 - $980,000) to help fund your retirement. However, you must also pay capital gains tax on the sale of your house.

Remember that the value of your house in figure 5.3 was $350,000. If we assume that you paid $300,000 for this house, then the capital gain would be $1,400,000 (the sale price) - $300,000 (the cost), or $1.1 million. You are currently allowed a $500,000 exception for capital gains on a primary residence in which you have lived for at least two of the last five years. Thus, the capital gain is reduced to $600,000, and the capital gains tax at the present rate of 15% would be $90,000.

The $420,000 that you have freed up from the sale of the house must be reduced by this $90,000. Therefore, you end up with a net of $330,000.

If we use the figure of $330,000 in figure 9.4 instead of $1.4 million, the adjusted asset total at retirement would be about $3.5 million, which is well below the amount needed to pay for your retirement. Of course, you would still have the new house as an asset, but it would not be available to fund your retirement. Clearly, selling your house and buying a new one is not feasible at this level of assets, unless you are willing to reduce your standard of living below what you had originally contemplated.

Therefore, there are at least three other scenarios that must be considered, including taking out a reverse mortgage, selling your house and renting something else, or paying for rent out of your retirement income.

A reverse mortgage may have some appeal, because a bank or other institution will pay you a monthly amount in the form of a loan for as long as you live in your home, based on the value of your house and the equity you have created. With the reverse mortgage, you could stay in your house, and you would receive a regular payment to help you reach your retirement income goal.

The loan must be repaid out of the sale of the house when you die or sell the house, and that money will reduce the value of your estate to your heirs. The Federal Trade Commission suggests that "reverse mortgages can help homeowners who are house-rich but cash-poor stay in their homes and still meet their financial obligations."[3] While the rate you earn on this asset might be somewhat less than your objective for the investment portfolio as a whole, most of your assets are working for you. This is not the case with the first alternative above.

Selling your house and paying rent may be appealing as a second alternative, and the rent could be financed from some of the income earned on the proceeds of the sale. With this option, you would probably still have more than $4.2 million at retirement. The net proceeds from the sale of your real estate would be invested with the Pay Yourself First assets in the way I will suggest in the next chapter

A third alternative is to pay any rent required out of your assumed retirement income. Remember that the $75,000 to which the multiple in figure 8.1 was applied already included a mortgage payment for the existing house. Since your house is now mortgage-free, the percentage of income that had gone to the mortgage can now go to pay rent. In this case, the full net value (after capital gains) of the real estate would be available to help fund your retirement, and the proceeds would be invested as in the second alternative.

I will assume that with one of these alternatives you can provide for an adequate living environment without compromising the assets you will need to generate the income in retirement that you have specified.

Impact of Variability of Returns

There is one potential problem with your projection for the level of both pre-retirement and post-retirement assets that is unavoidable, and that is that there is variability in the projected returns.

Remember from chapter 2 that the historical data for returns were presented in a range that was based on a standard statistical measure which described what happened two-thirds of the time.

As shown in figure 2.5, for example, the average return for bonds for all ten-year periods from 1935–2006 was 5.4%, but the range of ten-year annualized results two-thirds of the time was 2% to 9%. Similarly, the average return for stocks was 11.2%, but the range of ten-year results was 6% to 17% two-thirds of the time.

Projected returns also have a range of possible outcomes two-thirds of the time, and the projected annual return of 7%, which we have assumed for the pre-retirement period, is expected to fall in the middle of this range.

The range exists because of the uncertainty about the path of returns for bonds and stocks and for the combinations of bonds and stocks I am recommending you use for long-term investment planning in chapter 11.

The likely range of ten-year annualized returns at retirement for a portfolio that has an average asset allocation of 25% bonds and 75% stocks is 5.9% to 8.1%, again two-thirds of the time. Of course, as was mentioned in chapter 2, the range of returns is defined in such a way that there is one chance in six that the return could either be lower or higher than this range. To put it another way, five times out of six, the return will be in excess of 5.9%.

The range in total assets that you can expect at retirement based on this range of projected asset growth rates is shown in figure 9.5, in which the projected asset growth rate of 7% is in the middle of the figure. Of course, the assets at retirement for the projected asset growth rate of 7% are the same as those shown in figure 9.4.

Figure 9.5
Total Assets Available at Retirement ($)
Based on Projected Asset Growth Rates

	Projected Asset Growth Rate (%)		
	5.9	7.0	8.1
Tax-Deferred 401(k)	1,530,000	1,960,000	2,540,000
Real Estate	1,400,000	1,400,000	1,400,000
Pay Yourself			
-$200 per Paycheck for Thirty-five Years	560,000	720,000	950,000
-$200 More per Paycheck for Twenty-five Years	275,000	330,000	390,000
-$200 More per Paycheck for Fifteen Years	115,000	130,000	140,000
	950,000	1,180,000	1,480,000
TOTAL	3,880,000	4,540,000	5,420,000

As you can see, there is a very broad range of possible assets at retirement, based on the range of expected returns. The assets could range from about $3.9 million to $5.4 million. At first glance, this broad range may seem both surprising and discouraging. You might do everything right, and you would still end up with assets at retirement at the bottom of the range.

However, you must keep two things in mind: (1) You have to invest in bonds and stocks to even come close to what you will need at retirement. As I have mentioned several times, you have no choice. Cash investments, which do not have the variability of stocks and bonds, will not get you what you need. (2) $3.9 million is not an unacceptable result. You could sell your house and rent another property with some of your retirement income (one of the options suggested above), and you would still have enough to fund your retirement at a level close to the 80% you have specified.

My purpose in pointing all this out is to emphasize that, although we are typically dealing with projected returns in long-term investment planning, it is important to realize that results could be quite different than what you expect and still be within a reasonable range of probability. The important thing is to dimension this range, as I have done above, so that you can see what the risk of not achieving your objective actually is and what, if anything, you can do about it.

Other Retirement Alternatives

So far, we have been assuming that you will retire at age 65. There are two other possibilities that must be considered, and they are: (1) the possibility that you will work during retirement, and (2) the possibility that you will choose to work longer before you retire. In the first case, income earned in retirement would reduce the amount of the payments in each year below the amount for which you have provided.

In the second case, the retirement period would be shorter, requiring fewer years of payments. It is interesting to note that, according to the 2007 *Wall Street Journal* Financial Planning Survey, 38% of those in households with investment assets of at least $250,000 are expected to work past 65.[4]

It seems that retirees are increasingly doing one or both of these things, and either would clearly improve the ability to provide for retirement income. Given the shrinking number of actual workers projected to be available to support retirees, public policy may turn to encouraging one or both of these aspects.

Alternative Replacement Ratios

I mentioned earlier in the chapter that I would discuss briefly alternative income replacement ratios, the assets required for them and the resulting payment streams. The required $4.2 million in assets at retirement, developed in figure 9.1, will cover the projected payment stream, starting at $234,000 and growing at the assumed inflation rate of 3%. However, what if the assets do not reach the $4.2 million level? What happens if they are only, say, $3.0 million?

In this case, the assets are not going to be sufficient to meet the projected payment stream. There are only two alternatives to deal with this situation: (1) maintain the same payment schedule, starting at $234,000 and increasing at an inflation rate of 3%, and expect to run out of money at some point before the end of the thirty-year retirement period, or (2) reduce the payment stream so that the reduced payments, also increasing at an inflation rate of 3%, can be covered by the $3.0 million in available assets.

If the payment schedule is maintained, you will run out of assets in the eighteenth year. An eighteen-year planning horizon may be satisfactory, but it is not clear what you would use for income if you live longer than that.

On the other hand, if you reduce the payment schedule, the $3.0 million would cover a payment stream for thirty years, adjusted for 3% inflation, which begins at only $166,000. This represents about a 30% reduction from what you estimate to be your required starting payment in retirement ($234,000). It is about a 45% reduction from the income you are expecting to make in the final year before retirement.

In fact, neither option is acceptable, which means that $3.0 million is not acceptable. There are only two things you can do to avoid this situation: (1) maximize your contribution to your 401(k), maximize the match, and build a large pool of assets growing on a tax-deferred basis, and (2) pay yourself first as much as you can, as soon as you can.

Figure 9.6 summarizes what we have learned so far and what a 100% replacement ratio would require.

Figure 9.6
Required Assets at Retirement ($ million)
at Projected Inflation Rate of 3% and
Projected Asset Growth Rate in Retirement of 6.5%

	Replacement Rate		
	<u>55%</u>	<u>80%</u>	<u>100%</u>
Required Assets	3.0	4.2	5.3

The $3.0 million in assets at retirement represents the 55% replacement rate discussed above using the assumptions for the inflation rate and the asset growth rate we have used before. The $4.2 million is what was developed above for an 80% replacement ratio.

Finally, a 100% replacement ratio would require $5.3 million in assets at retirement, which represents about a 25% increase in required assets compared to the 80% replacement level. It demonstrates how much of your income in excess of 80% you can replace as you are successful in building your assets at retirement above the $4.2 million required for an 80% replacement ratio.

Dollar-Cost Averaging

Making regular investments, such as Pay Yourself First or contributions to your 401(k), allows you to take advantage of a phenomenon called "dollar-cost averaging." What this means is that you can end up with a larger investment amount by making regular investments over time than you would if you invested at the average price over the period.

How dollar-cost averaging works is illustrated in figure 9.7.

Figure 9.7
Dollar-Cost Averaging

	Period				
	<u>1</u>	<u>2</u>	<u>3</u>	<u>4</u>	<u>5</u>
Share Price($)	10	9	10	9	12

Amount Invested($)	100	100	100	100	100
Shares Purchased	10.00	11.11	10.00	11.11	8.33

Average Share Price($)	10.00
Shares Purchased at Average Unit Price	50.00
Shares Actually Purchased	50.55
Value of Investment at Average Price($)	600.00
Value of Actual Investment($)	606.60

Figure 9.7 assumes that the price of a share of stock fluctuates over a period of five years from $9 to $12. There are two investment alternatives presented: (1) investments of $100 each are made at the end of each year at the average price for the period, or (2) the shares purchased each year are equal to the same $100 investment for each year divided by the price for that year.

- The average share price is equal to the sum of the year-end prices ($50) divided by the number of years (five), or $10.
- If you used your total investment of $500 to purchase shares at this average price, you would have purchased 50.00 shares. The value of this investment at the end of year five would be equal to 50.00 shares times the price at the end of year five ($12), or 50.00 × $12 = $600.00.
- If, instead, you made regular investments of $100 at the end of each year and purchased whatever number of shares you could buy with that investment, you would have purchased 50.55 shares. The value of this investment at the end of year five would be 50.55 shares times the price at the end of year five, or 50.55 × $12 = $606.60.

The bottom line is that if you follow a dollar-cost averaging program, you will end up, in this example, with about 1% more shares (50.55 versus 50.00) and therefore 1% more in investment value ($606.60 versus $600.00) at the end of year five than if you had invested at the average price for the full five-year period. Dollar-cost averaging works regardless of the pattern of stock prices, and its success is not dependent on the particular pattern of year-end prices shown in figure 9.7.

Over the long period of time with which we are concerned for pre-retirement investing, the advantage can be considerable. This is obviously another strong reason for implementing the regular investment programs that I have been urging.

Taxes

What taxes will you have to pay on the assets you are accumulating for retirement during the pre-retirement period, and what taxes will you pay in retirement as you draw down these assets?

There are three asset categories in the accumulation period. The 401(k) assets are, by definition, tax-deferred, and so there is not tax due on them during this period. Your real estate is also a tax-deferred asset, because you do not pay taxes until you sell the property. If this is done for the first time when you retire, then the tax implications of a sale at retirement are those discussed above. The rate you pay is the capital gains tax rate, which is currently 15%.

You are creating the Pay Yourself First portfolio with after-tax dollars, so you, of course, are not taxed on them. Like your real estate, you would only be taxed on any capital gains on your portfolio you realize along the way. The investment program that I will recommend in the next chapter may generate some small capital gains income from time-to-time, but the impact on the taxes you pay will likely be quite small.

This portfolio does, however, generate ordinary income on a regular basis from dividends and interest on which you will have to pay taxes out of your income during the accumulation period. I have assumed that the dividend rate for your stock portfolio is 2% and that the yield on your fixed income portfolio is 5%.

This tax impact is very small in the early years and can be covered out of your salary for two reasons: (1) the portfolio is rapidly growing, but it is not very large during this period, and (2), as I will suggest in chapter 11, a very high percentage of the portfolio should be invested in stocks in the early years. As indicated above, the yield on stocks is much smaller than the yield on bonds and therefore will have less of an impact.

However, as time goes by during the accumulation period, the asset mix between fixed income and stocks changes gradually toward fixed income, which increases the amount of taxable income from this portfolio. As you will see in chapter 11, this is entirely appropriate.

There are two ways to address the problem of taxes on the income from your Pay Yourself First portfolio during the accumulation period. First, you can plan to pay the taxes out of the assets in the portfolio, liquidating enough of them every year to cover the taxes due. This means that, in addition to paying tax on the income itself, you will pay capital gains tax on any appreciation in the amount liquidated.

If you choose this alternative, by the time you reach retirement, the assets in this portfolio, which you have available to fund your retirement, will have been reduced by about 15%.

The other alternative is to plan to pay as much of the tax on income as you can out of your own salary, avoiding capital gains tax on amounts that would have been withdrawn and preserving the assets in the portfolio for retirement. If you can afford it, this is by far the best alternative. How much would the taxes be on the portfolio income?

To answer this question, you have to make certain assumptions. I think the following are reasonable and appropriate: (1) as indicated above, the yields on fixed income and stocks are 5% and 2%, respectively, (2) the portfolio gradually increases over time, based on the contributions specified earlier for the Pay Yourself First portfolio and the reinvested income, (3) the asset allocation gradually shifts towards fixed income, as outlined in chapter 11, and (4) the total tax rate you pay on any income from the portfolio is 30%.

Based on these assumptions, the taxes payable would gradually increase so that: (1) in year ten, they would be about $500, (2) in year twenty, they would be about $2,200, (3) in year thirty, they would be about $7,000, and (4) at retirement in thirty-five years, they would be about $11,000. It would seem that at least until age 60 (year thirty), it would be reasonable to assume that the taxes could be paid out of other income and that the growing Pay Yourself First portfolio could be preserved for retirement.

After that point, it may be more difficult to pay the taxes due out of other income, but if you started paying taxes by liquidating part of the portfolio, the impact on the size of the portfolio at retirement would be very small.

What about taxes in retirement? At this point, your taxes payable would be calculated as follows: (1) you would be taxed on all of the payments you receive from your 401(k), because your contributions and the income they have created have never been taxed before, (2) you would pay taxes on the income from your Pay Yourself First portfolio and the assets you have contributed from the sale of your house, but not on the principal, because the contributions to this portfolio have all been after-tax.

If your income in the year before retirement is the $292,500 and the income tax rate you pay is 30%, then the income tax in that final year would be about $88,000. Your after-tax income would therefore be about $205,000. What would the comparable figures be for your retirement income of $234,000?

The amount withdrawn from the tax-deferred assets would be roughly proportional to their weight in figure 9.4. These assets amount to about 43%, and thus the amount withdrawn from the tax-deferred assets would be about $106,000 (0.43 times $234,000). The tax on this amount at 30% would be about $32,000.

Only the income from the portfolio you create by combining your Pay Yourself First portfolio and the proceeds of the sale of real estate would be taxable. The tax on this portfolio would be about $24,000 in the first year of retirement. Thus, the total taxes due on the retirement income of $234,000 would be about $56,000, and the after-tax income would be $178,000.

Note that the reduction of 13% in after-tax income from the pre-retirement level of $205,000 is not as much as the reduction in pre-tax income. This is because part of the income you get in retirement is a return of after-tax money you invested to build the non-401(k) total assets shown in figure 9.4. To summarize, the reduction in after-tax income is less than the 20% reduction in pre-tax income from $292,500 to $234,000.

In short, you will be better off in retirement from an after-tax standpoint than you thought you would be when you determined that you needed 80% of your pre-tax, pre-retirement income, adjusted for inflation in your retirement years.

Review

I think it would be helpful to review the key assumptions that have produced the result shown in figure 9.4:

- A 401(k) plan based on a 4% contribution by you, plus a 4% match by your company
- Existing retirement assets of $50,000
- Pay Yourself First at the starting rate of $200 per paycheck, increased to $400 per paycheck after ten years and to $600 per paycheck after twenty years until age 65
- A rate of inflation in the value of your house of 4% per year
- A rate of return on your tax-deferred and Pay Yourself First assets of 7% per year in the years before retirement
- A rate of return of 6.5% per year in the retirement years
- A 3% rate of inflation in both the pre-retirement and post-retirement periods

I think that these are reasonable and representative assumptions, but they are no more than assumptions. Thirty-five years until retirement is a long time, and there is almost an infinite number of things that could happen that would change the assumptions. However, if you are going to develop a plan for retirement income, you have to have a set of assumptions such as these about key issues. You have no choice.

Remember that we have assumed that there will be no contribution from Social Security and from a defined benefit pension plan. If either is available to you at retirement, obviously that will help. Furthermore, we have not incorporated the benefit of working in retirement.

Given how difficult it is to forecast the future, the best course of action is to start out with as reasonable a set of assumptions as you can develop and the structure I have outlined here for dealing with them. This gives you confidence that you are as well prepared as you can be for the future and that you will be able to make the inevitable and necessary adjustments to the assumptions as time goes by, analyze their impact in terms of the structure, and take appropriate actions to deal with them.

The remaining question, as indicated at the outset of this chapter, is how do you establish an investment program that will allow you to produce a compound annualized return of 7% in your working years and 6.5% in retirement. This is the subject of chapter 10 and chapter 11.

Bottom Line

- The asset total at retirement required to provide the income you require during retirement, adjusted for a 3% rate of inflation in retirement, is a very large number by today's standards.
- The required assets are a function of: (1) the required income at the start of retirement, (2) the inflation rate, (3) the number of years you assume for the retirement period, and (4) the projected asset growth rate during retirement.
- The assumption is that the calculated required assets will just be sufficient to last for the retirement period, at the end of which they will be exhausted.
- Your tax-deferred assets in total might provide, say, 45% of the required assets at retirement and the value of your real estate might provide another 30%.
- The Pay Yourself First investment portfolio must then contribute the final 25%. This is the portfolio you have to create through your own savings.
- If you do not start paying yourself first a significant amount of your paycheck and increasing this amount periodically, you will be in the position described by Tennessee Williams in the quotation at the beginning of this chapter.
- While you may not be living in poverty, as Scott Cook suggests at the beginning of chapter 8, you will have to accept either: (1) a significant reduction in your standard of living in retirement, (2) a significant reduction in the portion of your retirement period that can be covered by the available assets, or (3) both.
- There is uncertainty around any projected returns for bonds, stocks, and the combinations of these assets that I am recommending in chapter 11. It is important to be aware of this variability and to make whatever adjustments you can to your investment planning to deal with it.
- You may decide to work longer than age 65 or to work in retirement, or both. Either of these choices will enable you to contribute more to your asset pool and may somewhat reduce the required payments in retirement and therefore the assets required for these payments.

- It is likely that you can pay the taxes due on the interest and dividends from the growing Pay Yourself First portfolio out of other income, so that you don't have to reduce this portfolio to pay these taxes.
- Your after-tax income in retirement should be more than you would expect, based on the 20% reduction in pre-tax income from the level immediately preceding retirement that you determined was necessary in retirement.
- Based on reasonable assumptions about asset growth rates, inflation, likely variability of returns, and Pay Yourself First amounts, there is a good chance that you can create an amount of assets at retirement that will provide a payment stream for a retirement period of thirty years, adjusted for expected inflation, which represents a replacement ratio of 80% of your income at retirement.

Chapter 10

Selecting Long-Term Investments and Estimating Expected Returns and Risks for Those Investments

The general systems of money management [today]
require people to pretend to do something they
can't do and like something they don't. It's a funny
business because on a net basis, the whole investment
management business together gives no value added to
all buyers combined.

Charles Munger
Warren Buffet's Partner

At the beginning of chapter 8, I outlined three questions that have to be answered in order to design an investment program that will help you achieve one of your Category One objectives—namely, income security in retirement. The first two questions were addressed in chapter 8 and chapter 9, respectively. Addressing the third question, How do you establish the investment program that will give you the best chance of having what you need when you retire? is the subject of this chapter and chapter 11.

My objectives for chapters 10 and 11 to enable you to address the third question are:

- To provide you with a framework to make the necessary projections for the expected long-term rates of return for bonds and stocks, the basic assets that I recommend you use in long-term investment programs,
- To identify the principal alternatives for investing in these assets,
- To describe how to use one of these alternatives in long-term investment programs for pre-retirement, retirement, and college saving to achieve your objectives for them.

The first two objectives will be covered in chapter 10, and the third will be covered in chapter 11.

Historical returns and risks for bonds and stocks in particular were discussed at length in chapter 2, and it would be helpful to review at least the Bottom Line for that chapter at this point.

Expected Rates of Return for Bonds and Stocks

As you recall from chapter 2, short term investments, such as money market funds, are appropriate for reserve assets but not for long-term investment programs. Real estate is already the largest investment most people have, and therefore there is no need to consider additional real estate in a long-term investment program. The assets with which we have to be concerned are bonds and stocks.

Over the long-term, investors in bonds typically get a return that is equal to the coupon (the fixed interest payment) on the bonds when they make their investment. If, for example, an investor purchases a newly issued thirty-year U.S. government bond for $1,000, and this bond has a coupon of 5%, then the investor will get an annual payment of $50.00 per year ($25.00 every six months) for the life of the bond.

Over the thirty years, therefore, an investor will get a return of 5% ($50.00 coupon divided by the $1,000 purchase price), and the U.S. government will pay back the principal you originally invested at the maturity date of the bond. Price fluctuations due to changes in interest rates in the interim will not matter.

Given that current long-term rates are approximately 5%, we can project a return of 5% from holding long-term bonds over a thirty- to thirty-five-year period.

Now let's turn to stocks. The long-term return for the stock market as a whole should be equal to the sum of the current yield and the expected long-term growth in dividends (yield + growth). The current yield is equal to the current dividend in dollars for an index of the stock market, based on the S&P 500 Index or the broader Russell 3000 Index, divided by the current value of the index. For example, if the dividend for the index is $2 and the stock market index is priced at $100, then the current yield is 2% (2/100).

Over long periods of time, the growth in dividends (the second component above) should be equal to the long-term growth in the economy, which in turn is equal to the sum of real growth and inflation. This assumes that corporate profit margins and dividend payout ratios (how much of their earnings companies pay to shareholders) do not change.

The first assumption is generally true, but the second is more problematic. There have been decade-long shifts in dividend payout ratios, and these shifts are unpredictable. The best you can do is to assume that whatever the current dividend payout ratio is will be constant.

Based on this discussion, we can make a forecast for the long-term return on stocks. In the current environment, long-term real growth is expected to be about 3%, and inflation, as discussed in chapter 8, is also expected to be about 3%. The current yield on the stock market as a whole is about 2%. Consequently, a reasonable forecast for the long-term return for stocks is 8% (3% + 3% + 2%).

These return projections for bonds and stocks are not the same as the historical returns presented in chapter 2. Recall that the long-term (1926–2006) returns for bonds and stocks were 5.4% and 10.4%, respectively (figure 2.1). The historical return for bonds is close to the return which can be projected at this point based on the current interest rate.

However, the projected return for stocks of 8% is significantly below the historical return. The difference can be calculated based on the equation above. Inflation and real growth were roughly 3% historically. The starting yield, however, was 4%. Therefore, the historical return was about 10% (3% + 3% + 4%). Clearly, the starting yield today is different, and that difference is primarily the difference in the historical and the projected rates of return for stocks.

Based on the projections developed here for the returns for bonds and stocks, we can calculate what the returns would be for various combinations of the two. For example, a 25/75 combination of bonds and stocks would produce a return of a little over 7%. This is approximately the assumed average asset allocation for the thirty-five-year period before retirement, as will be outlined in chapter 11. I have used a return of 7% in the pre-retirement period.

If, on the other hand, the allocation were 65/35 (bonds/stocks), then the long-term expected return would be somewhat more than 6.0%. This is the average allocation that is assumed for the retirement period of thirty years, also as outlined in chapter 11. I have used a long-term return for this period of 6.5%.

Investment Alternatives for Bonds and Stocks

Bonds can either be held outright (you own them individually) or in a mutual fund. The advantage of holding bonds outright is that you will get your money back at maturity, and you directly control what happens to this particular investment in the interim. That is, you can sell your bond whenever you wish, and you always know what the gain or loss is. Of course, there are no management fees.

The advantages of holding them in a mutual fund are that: (1) you get diversification, because your fund holds a broad range of bonds, (2) you get professional management, which is an advantage because it is difficult for you to make credit and value judgments about individual bonds, and (3) they can be included in an investment vehicle such as I will recommend in chapter 11. As you will see, I think that the latter is preferable.

Recall what I said about the importance of fees in the discussion about money market funds in chapter 4. As a general rule, all mutual funds that operate within a specific sector of the fixed income market are presented by the market with the same gross returns. What matters to you is the net return, and the difference is fees. By definition, those funds with lower fees will generally have better returns. A good example of this is provided in a recent Vanguard report about its fixed income funds, shown in figure 10.1. [1]

Figure 10.1
Vanguard vs. Competitors
As of 1/31/07

Type of Fund	Fee as a % of Assets Managed			Long-Term Performance (%)		
	Competitors	Vanguard	Difference	Vanguard	Competitors	Difference
Short-Term						
Treasury	0.58	0.26	0.32	4.9	4.2	0.70
Intermediate						
Treasury	0.69	0.26	0.43	6.1	5.9	0.20
Long-Term						
Treasury	0.69	0.26	0.43	7.4	5.9	1.50
GNMA	1.03	0.21	0.82	5.9	5.1	0.80

GNMA is the Government National Mortgage Association, an organization that guarantees investors the payment of interest and principal on mortgage-backed securities that are backed by loans which are federally insured or guaranteed. It is the only such organization to carry the full faith and credit guarantee of the U.S. government.

In every one of the fund types shown in figure 10.1, Vanguard has a significant fee advantage over its competitors. If what I said above about gross returns being the same in individual sectors is true, this fee advantage should translate into performance that is better than that of its competitors. You can see in the second half of figure 10.1 that this is the case. While the relationship is not necessarily one-for-one, in every case the Vanguard funds outperform their respective competitors.

The bottom line is that when you invest in fixed income funds, you want to invest with an organization that has low fees. When this is the case, your net return will almost always be higher than that of other funds because of the low fees.

However, just because you have low fees does not mean that you will outperform an index of a particular market sector. In the same Vanguard report,[2] the data shown in figure 10.2 are presented.

Figure 10.2
Vanguard and Competitors versus Indexes

Type of Fund	Long-Term Performance (%) (Ten Years Ended 1/31/07)			Performance Differences (%) Versus Indexes (Ten Years Ended 1/31/07)	
	Vanguard	Competitors	Relevant Index	Vanguard	Competitors
Short-Term Treasury	4.9	4.2	5.0	-0.1	-0.8
Intermediate Treasury	6.1	5.9	6.2	-0.1	-0.3
Long-Term Treasury	7.4	5.9	7.6	-0.2	-1.7
GNMA	5.9	5.1	5.9	0.0	-0.8

You can see that even with very low fees, every Vanguard fund, except for GNMA, has underperformed its respective index, although the underperformances are modest. The competitors, of course, have done even worse, because of the difference in fees shown in figure 10.1. The point is that it is very difficult to do better than an index in managing fixed income portfolios even with a big-fee advantage. Therefore, it follows that when investing in fixed income mutual funds, you want to invest in index funds with low fees.

In general, the alternatives for investing in stocks include: individual stocks, actively managed mutual funds, ETFs, or index funds. How do you decide which of these alternatives to select?

In my opinion, most individual investors are not well-served holding individual stocks, because

- they do not have enough information to perform as well as institutional investors in investing in individual stocks, which is what I was doing for forty years. Institutional investors always have more information than individual investors, and therefore these investors are at an information disadvantage. In fact, some of the most useful techniques used by institutional investors in selecting individual stocks in which to invest are based on individual investors making the same mistakes over and over.
- there is too much risk in holding a small number of stocks, as many investors do. This is because, while you might make some money

from time-to-time, you can always lose a lot of money as a result of a lack of diversification. Poor performance by one stock can significantly negatively affect your entire portfolio.

Therefore, it follows that you should hold diversified portfolios of stocks, which you buy in the form of mutual funds that invest in stocks (typically referred to as equity mutual funds). The institutional managers of these portfolios (called "active" managers) try to outperform certain institutional, broad-market benchmarks, such as the S&P 500 Index or the Russell 3000 Index. For you, the investor, this situation presents two problems.

The first problem with the institutional managers is that the vast majority of them consistently underperform their chosen benchmarks because of high management fees charged to the funds and the high cost of trading their portfolios because they have high turnover rates.

David Swensen, the highly respected chief investment officer of the Yale University Endowment Fund, provides some perspective: "A miniscule 4% of funds produce market-beating after-tax results with a scant 0.6 percent (annual) margin of gain. The 96% of funds that fail to meet or beat the Vanguard 500 Index Fund lose by a wealth-destroying margin of 4.8% per annum."[3]

If equity mutual funds typically underperform the markets in which they invest, the answer is to invest in the markets themselves through equity index funds. These funds are considered to be "passive", because the managers have as their objective to match the return of the index, rather than trying to outperform it, as is the case with "active" managers. The managers of index portfolios can come very close to matching index returns, because they typically own all or most of the stocks in the index and they have very low fees and portfolio turnover.

Fund management fees are as important in equity investing as they are in investing in bonds, and it may surprise you to know that there is a wide difference in fees just for index funds investing in stocks. "The gap between the costs charged by the low-cost funds and the high-cost funds offered by ten major fund organizations for their S&P 500 Index–based funds runs upward of an amazing 1.2 percentage points per year."[4]

An index fund is designed to track a broad market index. Why would you pay more than you have to in order to achieve the same gross return that all of the funds in this category provide? "The wise investor will select only those index funds that are available without sales loads, and those operating with the lowest costs."[5]

The second problem is that most investors time their purchases of equity mutual funds in counterproductive ways, buying high (in the late 1990s, for example) and selling low (in the summer of 2002, for example). This activity significantly reduces the return they actually receive from what they would have received if they had simply bought and held throughout the period.

Research from Dalbar, a financial services research firm, actually quantifies the loss to the average investor due to counter-productive timing efforts. "For a $10,000 investment [made] over twenty years, dollar-cost averaging [making a constant investment on a periodic basis, such as monthly] produced 40% higher returns than those earned by the average investor chasing returns."[6]

Let's be clear about what Dalbar is saying. If your strategy is to make semimonthly or monthly investments, which is what I am suggesting with Pay Yourself First, you will end up 40% better off over time than if you try to time your investments. This is a profound conclusion, and it is critically important to incorporate in your funding strategy to achieve your objective of retirement income security.

The only way to avoid this problem is to do what Warren Buffet suggested at the outset of chapter 2. Put your portfolio on intelligent autopilot, as described in chapter 11, and don't try to time purchases and sales.

In recent years, a new form of investing in equity index funds has been created. This is the exchange traded fund, or ETF. Like conventional index funds, index ETFs buy all the stocks in a particular index and try to match the return of the index. One major difference is that the ETF is traded on a stock exchange just like an individual stock.

This means that you can buy and sell them at any time the market is open, as opposed to just buying at the close, as is the case with conventional mutual funds. ETFs are growing much faster than conventional mutual funds, and the assets in ETFs have grown to approximately $450 billion in just three years.

Should you consider ETFs for your long-term investment programs in place of conventional equity index funds? I think that the answer is no, and following are some of the reasons:

- The majority of ETFs that have been created are not designed to replicate a broad market index, which is the basic building block of a long-term equity investment program. They are designed to track much more narrow indexes. However, index ETFs could be an option.

- One of the presumed advantages of ETFs is that they offer better liquidity, because they are tradable instantaneously, than conventional index funds, which are only priced once per day. However, this cannot be viewed as a big plus, even if you bought index ETFs, if the objective is to buy and hold an index fund to take full advantage of the return that the stock market offers over the long-term.

- ETFs claim to have advantages over conventional index funds because of lower expenses and lower taxes related to turnover. However, according to a study by Morningstar, a research firm, commissioned by the *Wall Street Journal*, "big, low-cost index funds from Boston-based Fidelity Investments and Vanguard Group, Inc., Malvern, Pa. outperformed the [index] ETFs in most of the comparisons we set up. For the forty time periods studied, the mutual funds prevailed in thirty-four—including a sweep of the one-, three-, and ten-year after-tax categories." [7]

The four categories analyzed were "the Standard & Poor's 500 Index, the total U.S. stock market, international stock markets, and a broad-based bond index."

At this point, we can conclude that for investing in bonds and stocks you should invest in conventional, low-cost, low-turnover index funds. Bond and equity index funds give you the returns from these markets, which are critically important because they are the expected returns you used in the first place in making the projections required for estimating assets needed to fund your retirement.

John Bogle puts it this way: "While I can't say that classic indexing is the best strategy ever devised, your common sense should reassure you that the number of strategies that are worse is infinite." [8]

As indicated above, it is very difficult and not necessary to the projections for you to do better than the returns the markets provide through index funds.

In fact, almost anything you do other than invest in index funds is going to provide returns that are less than index returns and thus compromise your projections.

What about asset allocation? How much do I invest in bond and stock index funds? The answer depends on several considerations: (1) the return you are seeking and the risk you are willing to take to get it, and (2) the returns that formed the basis of the projections you want to make for retirement planning.

Without going into a lot of the assumptions involved, I think that most professional advisers would agree that an asset allocation of roughly 25% bonds and 75% stocks on average for the period during which assets are accumulating before retirement is reasonable. However, this means that the asset allocation would have to have more equities in the beginning and less at the end. During the retirement period, the asset allocation should average 60% bonds and 40% stocks, once again with more stocks at the beginning and less at the end.

The problem with asset allocation is that most people will not leave it alone. As indicated above, they will add to their stocks at the wrong time and vice versa, once again producing results that are almost always worse than what would have been produced if they had left the asset allocation alone.

The group for which I was responsible also successfully managed asset allocation products, but I can assure you that, even for professional investors, asset allocation is extremely difficult. As is the case with selecting individual stocks, I think individual investors are at a significant information disadvantage in asset allocation. For them, asset allocation is a fool's errand.

Bottom Line

- The long-term expected return for bonds is about 5%, which is equal to the current interest rate. This is somewhat below the actual long-term return for bonds from 1926–2006 of 5.4%.
- The long-term expected return for stocks is about 8%, which is less than the historical return of 10.4%. The difference is primarily related to the starting yield.
- An average combination of 25% bonds and 75% stocks in the pre-retirement period would produce about a 7% return, based on these assumptions, and an average combination of 60% bonds and 40%

stocks in the post-retirement period would produce a return of about 6.5%.

- For the purpose of developing the long-term investment programs outlined in chapter 11, bonds should not be purchased individually. They should only be purchased in low-fee, low-turnover bond index mutual funds.
- Stocks should not be purchased individually, because: (1) you do not have an information edge to make this worthwhile, and (2) there is too much volatility risk and exposure to the negative impact of individual stocks. In addition, they should not be purchased in ordinary equity mutual funds, because: (1) these funds on balance underperform their chosen benchmarks, and (2) the sales loads, base fees, and transaction costs significantly reduce returns. Stocks should only be purchased in low-cost, low-turnover stock index mutual funds.
- Individuals should not engage in their own asset allocation between bonds and stocks. Once again, they do not have enough information to do this to their advantage, and by trying to do so they will almost certainly seriously compromise their ability to achieve the returns they need to achieve their objective of retirement security.
- The solution I recommend to provide for investment in index funds and to deal with the problem of asset allocation is found in chapter 11.

Chapter 11

Establishing Long-Term Investment Programs for Pre-Retirement, Retirement, and College Saving

At the beginning of chapter 10, I indicated that I had three objectives to help you address the third major question from chapter 8: How do you establish the investment program that will give you the best chance of having what you need when you retire?

The first two objectives were covered in chapter 10. The third objective, which is the subject of this chapter, is to describe how to use one of these alternatives in long-term investment programs for pre-retirement, retirement, and college saving to achieve your objectives for them.

Long-Term Investment Program for Pre-Retirement

You might think that the long-term investment program for the pre-retirement period would end with retirement. At that point, the asset allocation would have become very conservative, because retirement is imminent and you cannot afford to take any risks and lose money. You would plan to live on the money you have accumulated, and you would have a very low exposure to stocks.

However, this should not be the case. In the first place, when you get to retirement age, you may have a life expectancy of twenty-five to thirty years, and you should plan for that possibility. In the second place, you may retire earlier than you expect to retire because you are in good financial health and can do something else for compensation that you have really wanted to do. In fact, the length of the retirement period could approach the length of the pre-retirement period.

What this situation suggests is that the pre-retirement and post-retirement periods are really part of one overall planning period, which could be as much as sixty-five years. In other words, your investment program must contemplate a continuum that stretches from the time you first start saving for retirement, at, say, age 30, all the way through your life. To be sure, there are two distinct periods—pre-retirement and post-retirement—but they must be linked together into an overall investment plan.

For a horizon like this, it is necessary to begin with a plan for asset allocation for the entire period. This plan should be based on the following general philosophy:

- As discussed in chapter 2, stocks are more risky than bonds, but they have a higher long-term return. It therefore makes sense to have a high exposure to stocks at the beginning of this investment horizon, when you can have a major loss and have the time horizon to recover. Correspondingly, the exposure to bonds should be low at the beginning.
- The exposure to stocks should decline gradually over time as your tolerance for risk goes down. That is, your ability to withstand major losses in your portfolio becomes less and less.
- The exposure to stocks should be low at the end of the planning horizon, and the bond exposure should be high. This is because your ability to withstand losses is very low at that time.

- The stock exposure at the end of the pre-retirement period should be consistent with the remaining portion of the investment planning horizon, which might be as much as thirty years or more. While you might not be able to withstand the volatility of stocks that you could tolerate when you started your investment program, you need to have a healthy exposure to equities to provide the return you will need to make your assets last throughout your retirement.

Figure 11.1 illustrates one example of how the asset allocation in your long-term investment plan could be designed to be consistent with this philosophy—your Lifetime Asset Allocation. There are other examples, but they are all variations on the same philosophy. Note the high stock exposure at 90% at the outset and how it stays at this level for the first fifteen years of the planning horizon.

Then, note how it declines over time to 20% at age 80 and stays at that level. Note also that in this example the stock allocation at the retirement age of 65, which we have been using for planning purposes, is still 50%. This is consistent with the idea that the planning horizon at this point could be another thirty years, and it demonstrates how the two periods are linked.

The exposure to bonds is the mirror image of the exposure to stocks, as it should be. The bond exposure starts at 10%, and then it rises to 80% at age 80 and stays at that level until the end of the planning horizon.

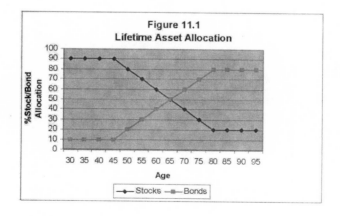

Remember that we have concluded that you want to use low-cost index funds to get the bond and stock exposures you want. Furthermore, we concluded that you do not want to be involved in asset allocation. How, then, do you get the exposures shown in figure 11.1?

In general, there are two approaches you can use: (1) balanced funds, and (2) target funds. Balanced funds typically either maintain a constant allocation between bonds and stocks or vary the asset allocation within ranges, based not on what you want to do but on what the managers believe will give them the best return. Target funds, which are sometimes called "lifestyle funds," vary the asset allocation from aggressive to conservative as your life progresses.

The asset allocation of a conventional balanced fund (40% bonds and 60% stocks) compared to the lifetime asset allocation from figure 11.1 is shown in figure 11.2. As you can see, the asset allocation over time for the balanced fund is effectively constant. As a result, compared to the lifetime asset allocation, the equity exposure is too low at the beginning of the period and too high at the end. Since the asset allocation does not change, this pattern of asset allocation over time is not consistent with the asset allocation philosophy outlined above. Therefore, for this reason in particular, balanced funds do not fit into the kind of long-term investment plans we are discussing.

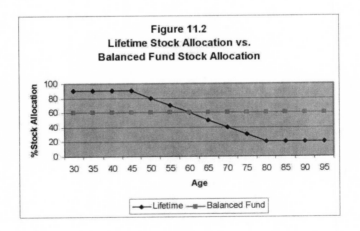

Figure 11.2
Lifetime Stock Allocation vs.
Balanced Fund Stock Allocation

To achieve the returns that you need to earn to make the projections for retirement in chapter 9 realistic, I recommend that you invest exclusively in target date funds. These funds have the following advantages, each of which was discussed above:

- You can choose a target fund with a date that corresponds to your complete investment horizon (both pre-retirement and retirement) and that has an asset allocation pattern which matches as closely as possible your chosen lifetime asset allocation plan.
- The target date fund sets an initial asset allocation that is appropriate for your time horizon, which would be heavily oriented to stocks. Then, the exposure to stocks is gradually reduced and the bond exposure is gradually increased as time goes by, as you get closer to the target date and as your tolerance for risk goes down.
- The target date fund should invest in bond and stock index funds.
- When the target date is reached, the fund will have a default asset allocation that typically will be much more oriented toward bonds than stocks, which will be maintained as long as you are invested in the fund.
- Through these arrangements, your investment program is on autopilot. You are investing in stocks and bonds to get the returns the markets provide, the asset allocation decisions are made by the fund manager in an appropriate and understandable way, and you are using low-cost index funds to give you the bond and stock exposures within the fund.
- Because of the nature of a target date fund and its underlying holdings, the fee you pay should be quite low, but this is not always the case. Use only target date funds that have what you want at low cost.

There are a number of organizations that provide target date funds, sometimes called "Life Cycle Funds," including American, Fidelity, T. Rowe Price, and Vanguard. The funds from all four organizations adjust the asset allocation as time goes by in favor of bonds and away from stocks.

In fact, according to the *Wall Street Journal*, "There are now 34 mutual-fund companies offering target-date funds, which have $144.5 billion in assets, according to Morningstar, Inc. The funds are getting a boost from the recent federal pension bill, under which target-date funds are expected to be default investment options for more 401(k) retirement plans."[1]

However, only the Vanguard funds use index funds and have very low fees, two of the critical requirements described above. The competitors' fee for these funds averages almost four times the Vanguard fee.

Figure 11.3 shows how the asset allocation in Vanguard's 2045 target date fund, for example, is expected to compare with the lifetime asset allocation shown in figure 11.1.

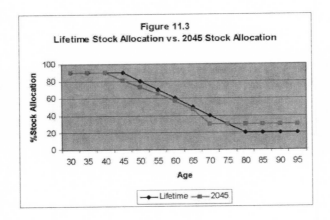

The asset allocation of the Target Fund 2045 matches the lifetime asset allocation pattern very closely until age 80. At that point, Target Fund 2045's asset allocation is at 30%, compared to 20% for the lifetime asset allocation. The difference then stays at that level.

What figure 11.3 demonstrates is that by investing in a single investment vehicle—Target Fund 2045 or another fund with a similar target date—from the time you start saving for retirement at age 30, you will get all the advantages of target date funds outlined above plus an asset allocation that changes over time and is consistent with your lifetime asset allocation. Your investment plan for your lifetime is truly on autopilot in an optimal way. You really do not have to do anything except make at least the required investments in the target date fund.

Let me emphasize this important point. You do not have to worry about picking stocks or specific mutual funds, because you are investing in low-cost index funds. You do not have to worry about asset allocation, because it is changing automatically over time in a way that is generally consistent with your long-term plan. Finally, the cost you pay for all this is very low compared to most alternatives.

The asset allocation in the Vanguard Target Fund 2045 starts at 90% in stocks and 10% in bonds. At the end of the pre-retirement period at age 65, the asset allocation in the fund is 50% stocks and 50% bonds. On average, the asset allocation in the pre-retirement period is about 80% stocks and 20% bonds. Using the long-term rates of return for stocks and bonds of 8% and 5% for bonds, respectively, the expected rate of return would be about 7.4%, compared to the assumption used in the long-term projections in chapter 9 of 7.0%.

On average, the asset allocation in the post-retirement period is about 35% stocks and 65% bonds. Using the long-term rates of return for stocks and bonds of 8% and 5%, respectively, the expected rate of return would be a little over 6%, compared to the assumption used in the long-term projections in chapter 9 of 6.5%

What happens if you did not or do not start contributing to your 401(k) and Pay Yourself First at age 30? It really is never too late to start, although your retirement objective may be harder to reach, depending on what you have been doing with your assets in the interim.

However, whenever you start, you should do exactly what I am recommending for those who do start early. Invest as much as you can as soon as you can in the Vanguard target date fund that gives you the lifetime asset allocation pattern shown in figure 11.1 that is appropriate from the time you either start making contributions for the first time or transfer assets from some other provider, or both. That is, get on a low-cost autopilot investment plan at the earliest possible moment.

For example, if you are 65 when you start your investment program, you want to use a Vanguard target date fund with an asset allocation at that time of about 50% stocks and 50% bonds. The asset allocation for the balance of your life would be similar to the asset allocation for Vanguard Target Fund 2045 over the same period. If you are 55 when you start your investment program, then you want to use a Vanguard target date fund that at that point would have an asset allocation of about 70% stocks and 30% bonds (see figure 11.1).

I would like to show you some of the characteristics of Vanguard's Target Fund 2045:

- The total fee is 0.21%, which is very low. Vanguard indicates that the fee for comparable competitive funds is 0.72%.[2]
- The minimum investment is $3,000.
- It has a ticker symbol, like individual stocks and funds—VTIVX—so you can monitor it by its ticker symbol.
- It shows up in newspapers under "TgtRe2045," so you can monitor its performance in print.
- Dividends and capital gains are distributed annually in December, which minimizes recordkeeping.
- As of April 30, 2007, the asset allocation was as shown in figure 11.4.[3] This allocation is in line with what you would expect from figure 11.3. The high exposure to equities creates considerable downside risk, but this is the kind of risk that can easily be tolerated and from which one can recover in a time frame this long.

Figure 11.4
Asset Allocation in
Vanguard 2045 Target Fund
as of 4/30/07 (%)

Stocks	89.9
Bonds	10.1
Total	100.0

The actual investments in the Target Fund 2045 as of April 30, 2007, are shown in figure 11.5.[4] As you can see, all of the underlying investments are index funds. Within the stock portion of the portfolio, there is exposure (almost 18% of the total portfolio) to markets in parts of the world outside the United States, which adds diversification and which may improve return and reduce risk.

Figure 11.5
Investments in Vanguard Target Fund 2045
As of 3/31/07

Fund	%
Total Stock Market Index Fund	71.9
European Stock Index Fund	10.5
Pacific Stock Index Fund	4.7
Emerging Markets Stock Index Fund	2.8
Total Bond Market Index Fund	10.1
	100.0

How Vanguard expects the asset allocation by type of fund to change over time is illustrated in figure 11.6.[5]

Figure 11.6
Expected Changes in Asset Allocation
Over Time in Vanguard Target Fund 2045

Fund	Date					Default
	2007	2017	2027	2037	2042	2047
Total Stock Market Index	72.0	72.0	66.0	53.3	40.0	24.0
European Stock Index	10.6	10.6	9.7	7.9	5.9	3.5
Pacific Stock Index	5.0	5.0	4.6	3.7	2.8	1.7
Emerging Markets Stock Index	2.4	2.4	2.2	1.8	1.3	0.8
Total Bond Market Index	10.0	10.0	17.5	33.3	40.0	45.0
Inflation-Protected Securities	0.0	0.0	0.0	0.0	10.0	20.0
Prime Money Market	0.0	0.0	0.0	0.0	0.0	5.0
	100.0	100.0	100.0	100.0	100.0	100.0

The asset allocation reaches the default level in 2047, and it stays at this point for the balance of your retirement unless you decide to do something to change it. These are the approximate asset allocations plotted in figure 11.3.

Note also the exposure to some inflation-protected securities and money market securities in later years, when these investments become more important. Inflation protected securities are fixed income securities specifically designed to protect against inflation, a particular concern as you get into later years. The money market securities are acting at this point as the reserve asset first described in chapter 2.

Hopefully, you can see what the nature of target date funds is and how they work. For all the reasons mentioned above, target date funds are the only investment vehicle I would recommend for most people. With everything on intelligent autopilot, all you have to do is to concentrate on meeting or exceeding the Pay Yourself First contribution to your particular target date fund. The rest will take care of itself.

It would be sufficient for you to stop at this point. You have successfully exposed yourself at low cost to the returns from the bond and stock markets, which is what you need to reach your desired level of retirement security. When you get to this point, you are extraordinarily better positioned than most people. However, there is one additional factor you may want to consider at some point, and that is the impact of taxes.

From an asset allocation standpoint, it makes sense to think of your tax-deferred 401(k) assets and your taxable (Pay Yourself First) assets as two separate pools. Given the tax rates today for ordinary income and capital gains, you want to try to have as much in stocks as possible in the taxable assets, so that capital gains, if any, are taxed at the maximum rate of 15%. You pay ordinary income tax on distributions from a 401(k), so the more stocks you have in your tax-deferred pool, the more you are transferring gains, which could be taxed at capital gains rates in your taxable portfolio, into income taxed at ordinary income tax rates when it comes out of your 401(k). Furthermore, you minimize the ordinary income taxation, because stocks have a lower yield than bonds.

On the other hand, you should have more bonds in your tax-deferred account, because otherwise you would be paying ordinary income taxes on the interest you are earning. You might as well postpone paying these taxes, which you will pay anyway at some point, as long as possible.

The solution to this problem is to choose different target date funds for your two pools of money, an approach that will help you distribute your assets in a tax-efficient way that will also maintain your overall allocation where you want it to be and where it needs to be. This works whenever you can buy a target date fund with more equity exposure than your current target. When this is the case, you could put some of your taxable assets in the target date fund with more stocks, and put more of your tax-deferred assets in a target date fund with a higher fixed income exposure. You just have to make sure that the weighted exposure of the two pools is equal to the overall target at that time.

However, when you start out, there is no alternative to using the same target date fund in both pools, because there is no target date fund with a higher equity exposure than the 90% in Target Fund 2045. This will be the case for at least the first fifteen to twenty years of your investment time horizon. Nevertheless, it is worth keeping in mind the potential improvement in tax efficiency you can make at some point.

The Long-Term Investment Program for Retirement

The long-term investment program for retirement, which at one point you might have considered a separate program, can now be seen as part of the continuum mentioned above, which includes the pre-retirement period. Reaching the assumed retirement age of 65 is an important point on the continuum, because this is the point at which you stop adding to your assets and start gradually liquidating them to support you in retirement.

However, it is only one point on the continuum that you have established and will have been following for many years. Thus, the long-term investment program for retirement is simply a continuation of what you have been doing.

According to figure 11.3, when you get to the assumed retirement age of 65, the asset allocation will be 50% stocks and 50% bonds. This is a reasonable starting asset allocation for the post-retirement period. If you stay with the asset allocation plan for Target Fund 2045, the asset allocation will fall to 30% stocks and 70% bonds at age 75, and then it stays at that level through age 95.

The lifetime asset allocation first developed in figure 11.1 suggests that you want to end up with an asset allocation with even less stocks and more bonds (20% stocks/80% bonds) toward the end of the period. If you did that, the average return over the period would be somewhat lower.

However, this only becomes a problem at age 80 and older, which is 50 years from now if you start your investment program today at age 30. That's a long time, and a variety of unanticipated things could have happened in the interim that would have affected your situation, both positively and negatively. I think that the best way to deal with this problem is to wait until you get there, see where you are compared to where you want to be in terms of available assets, and make a decision at that point.

The advantage of using target date funds is that you can always create an asset allocation that meets your objective for lower risk as the retirement period develops, while maintaining all the advantages of the target date funds discussed above. In some cases, this may require buying more than one target date fund to get the asset allocation and return/risk exposure that is appropriate for your lifetime asset allocation. This approach is illustrated in figure 11.7.

Figure 11.7
Tax Efficient Allocation of Assets
Between Tax-Deferred and Taxable Assets
for $1,000,000 Combined Portfolio

Type of Account	Total Account Assets $	Allocation to Fixed Income %	Account Assets in Fixed Income	Allocation to Stocks %	Account Assets in Stocks $
Tax-Deferred 401(k)	500,000	70	350,000	30	150,000
Taxable	500,000	10	50,000	90	450,000
Total	1,000,000	40	400,000	60	600,000

Figure 11.7 illustrates the possible composition of a $1 million portfolio with $500,000 each invested in a 401(k) and a taxable, Pay Yourself First portfolio. The 401(k) portfolio would be invested in a target date fund with an asset allocation of 70% in fixed income and 30% in stocks. The Pay Yourself First portfolio would be invested in a target date fund with an allocation of 10% to fixed income and 90% to stocks.

The resulting overall allocation would be 40% in fixed income and 60% in stocks. The asset allocations to particular target date funds could change over time, so that the overall allocation would match what you want it to be.

The allocation to target date funds with the allocations for each portfolio shown in figure 11.7 would be tax efficient in the way described above. The assets that would create the highest current income tax potential—the fixed income assets—would be mostly in the tax-deferred portfolio, and the assets with the smallest current income tax potential would be in the taxable portfolio.

The only problem with this approach is with potential capital gains tax on any gains when you switch from one target date fund to another to keep your overall asset allocation where you want it to be. This would not be a problem in the 401(k) in which all taxes are deferred. However, it would lead to capital gains in the Pay Yourself First portfolio. However, these would be taxed at the current low rate of 15%.

My assumption throughout this discussion has been that you plan to retire when you are 65. If you retire earlier, you will have to have more money than at 65, and if you retire later, the money you have accumulated will go farther.

Remember that I have assumed that you have two pools of invested assets: Pay Yourself First and 401(k). Regardless of when you start to withdraw funds to provide the retirement income you have projected, the question is, from which pool do you get the money? The general rule is that you should draw down your Pay Yourself First assets first. There are at least two reasons for this:

- The accumulated gains in your Pay Yourself First portfolio will be taxed at only the current capital gains rate, currently 15%, which is generally lower than most people pay on ordinary income. Money withdrawn from your 401(k) portfolio is taxed at ordinary income tax rates.
- The 401(k) assets are tax-deferred. The longer you can preserve the benefit of tax-deferred compounding, the more total after-tax income you will have in the end. Furthermore, if you have overestimated your needs in retirement and there are any assets left over to pass on to your heirs, it is possible for them to continue the tax deferral.

The only exception to the general rule is when you have reached age 70 1/2 and have to take mandatory distributions from your 401(k) under current law. In this case, you will want to use that money before taking funds from your Pay Yourself First account.

By putting your long-term investment programs for both the pre-retirement and retirement periods on autopilot, you are following the sage advice of John Bogle at the beginning of this chapter. In effect, you are putting yourself firmly and appropriately in a position to benefit from the long-term returns that the markets provide and "just standing there" to avoid upsetting the apple cart.

Annuities

There is another alternative for retirement planning that deserves mention, and that is an annuity. An annuity provides a payment structure that is the reverse of that of a mortgage. In the case of a mortgage, the financial institution provides you with the funds that represent the mortgage, and you pay the financial institution back over time. In the case of an annuity, you provide funds to an insurance company, and the insurance company will pay you a specified amount of money over a period of time and in a manner you specify.

Because they provide a specified sum and thus eliminate most of the uncertainty about retirement income that is present with a long-term investment program like the one described in the first part of this chapter, annuities are popular with certain people. According to research from Morningstar, Inc., and Limra International, an association of insurance and financial insurance companies, there were $1.9 trillion in annuity assets at the end of 2006.[6]

The different kinds of annuities are summarized in figure 11.8.

Figure 11.8
Types of Annuities

	Immediate	Deferred
Fixed	X	X
Variable	X	X

Annuities are either fixed or variable. Fixed annuities pay you a fixed amount of money for as long as you, or someone else, such as your spouse, live. Variable annuities pay you an amount which is a function of investment results produced from your choices from an array of investment alternatives provided by the insurance company, sometimes subject to a minimum. Annuities are either immediate or deferred. An immediate annuity is one that starts making payments immediately after you purchase the insurance contract from the insurance company. A deferred annuity provides you payments at some time in the future, typically when you retire.

Variable annuities are more popular than fixed annuities. In 2006, sales of variable annuities at about $160 billion were twice the sales of fixed annuities.[7] Of the $1.9 trillion in total annuity assets outstanding, about $1.4 trillion, or about 74%, were variable annuities.[8]

There is a variety of payment options and terms. You could choose a single life annuity, which will make payments to you as long as you live, or you could chose a joint and survivor annuity, which will make payments as long as you and, for example, your wife are alive. Regardless of which type of payment option you choose, you can choose to guarantee payments for a specified period, such as ten or twenty years. If you die before the guarantee period is up, the payments go to your beneficiaries until the end of the guarantee. If you are concerned about inflation, you can choose to have your payments adjusted for inflation.

Be aware that your payment schedules and any guarantees you choose are dependent on the financial soundness of the insurance company providing the annuity. After all, you still want the company to be in sound financial condition in thirty years.

What this means is that you should only consider annuities provided by a company that is highly rated by rating agencies such as Standard & Poor's or A.M. Best. Most insurance companies will provide ratings on their Web sites, or you can go directly to the Web sites of the rating agencies.

The income you receive from an annuity depends on a number of factors, including: the initial payment, your life expectancy based on standard tables, the payment options you select, current interest rates (if you choose a fixed annuity), and investment experience (if you choose a variable annuity).

Annuities can be expensive. In the first place, if you buy the annuity from an intermediary, such as an insurance agent, you are likely to pay a sales load or a commission. Commissions are higher for deferred than for immediate annuities. Secondly, you pay annual fees that average 2.5%, about 1% higher than the average fee for U.S. mutual funds, according to Morningstar.[9] Finally, there are significant penalties, or surrender charges, for deferred annuities if you decide that you do not want your annuity any more. These can range from single digits to as high as 20% in the early years, although they typically decline over time.

Why would someone buy an annuity? One of the primary reasons might be to provide a guaranteed income that will last for the rest of your life. Another might be to seek a tax-deferred buildup of the investment value inside a deferred annuity. Investment gains while the annuity is in force are not taxed. A third reason might be to provide some income security for a portion of your expenses, such as everyday bills. "Many financial planners recommend putting as much as 25% of your total nest egg in an annuity," specifically for this purpose. [10]

My recommendations about annuities are as follows:

- If you are extremely concerned about the security of income to cover some of your household expenses, it would make sense to use a small amount (10% to 20%) of the assets that you would otherwise devote to the investment program outlined in the first part of this chapter to purchase an immediate fixed annuity.
- Deferred annuities are investment programs in an insurance wrapper. In general, I think what I have said throughout this book about combining multiple elements in one program applies again in this case. While there are the advantages of tax-deferred buildup and the insurance wrapper, you pay a lot to get them.
- These advantages should be weighed against the fact that the investment options offered by the insurance company may not be what you want and the possibility that you could maintain your investment program and purchase insurance directly for less total cost. In this way, you would have transparency for your investment program and your insurance purchase. In a combination product like a deferred annuity, these two critical elements are hard to separate.

College Savings Plans

Once you have a plan for achieving your goal of retirement income security, as developed earlier in this chapter, it is time to think about funding a college savings plan for your children or grandchildren. There are three principal approaches you can use for saving for your child's education expenses in college

- 529 plans
- Coverdell Education Savings Accounts
- Uniform Gifts (or Transfers) to Minors

Plans such as 529 are sponsored by states (some states have more than one), and the assets are typically managed by a third party, such as a mutual fund management company. There are no income limits for contributions to 529 plans, and you control the investments. Many states provide for a tax deduction for contributions to the plan sponsored by the state in which you live. However, you can contribute to the plan in any state.

Contributions are limited by the annual standard gift tax exclusion amount, which is currently $12,000 per person, or $24,000 per person for married couples. Earnings from the 529 plan accumulate free from federal income tax, and withdrawals that are used for higher education expenses, such as tuition, fees, supplies, books, and equipment, are also free from federal income tax. If you use withdrawals for other purposes, the withdrawals may be taxable, and you may have to pay a 10% penalty.

Coverdell Education Savings Accounts may be used to save for expenses at any educational level—elementary, secondary, and college. Contributions are limited to $2,000 per beneficiary, and there are income limitations beyond which contributions are not permitted. Earnings grow free from federal income tax. Withdrawals must be made within 30 days of the beneficiary's thirtieth birthday, and accumulated income that is used for qualified expenses is not taxed.

Uniform Gifts to Minors Act (UGMA) or Uniform Transfers to Minors Act (UTMA) accounts can be used for anything that benefits the child, as opposed to being limited just for education, as is the case with the first two approaches. The same gift tax limitations apply as is the case in 529 plans. In the case of these two approaches, however, the child by law gains control of the assets at the age of majority (18 or 21) in most states. Earnings are taxed at either the child's tax rate or the parents' rate or both.

Figure 11.9 summarizes the provisions of each approach.

Figure 11.9
College Saving Options

	Contribution Limit	State	Federal		Allowable Uses
		Tax Deduction	Tax On Earnings	Tax On Withdrawals	
529 Plans	$12,000 or $24,000(1)	Yes (3)	No	No	Higher Education
Coverdell	$2,000(2)	No	No	No	Any Education
UGMA/ UGTA	$12,000 or $24,000(1)	No	Yes	No	Specified Uses Until Majority

(1) Limit for Married Couples
(2) Contribution Limit Phased Out
(3) In Most States

The 529 plan is the most rapidly growing and for good reasons: (1) it has the maximum contribution, (2) it allows for a tax deduction in most states, and (3) it is focused on higher education, the educational level that involves the largest educational expense for most people.

No matter which approach you use, the best investment program for a college savings program is also a target date fund. Since the time horizon for paying for college from the birth of your child is twenty to twenty-five years, you would choose a target date fund with roughly the same time horizon. In the case of the Vanguard target date funds, and if you were starting your 529 plan today, you would invest in Target Fund 2030. It currently has an asset allocation that is roughly 85% stocks and 15% bonds. By 2035, this fund should have an asset allocation of 70% bonds, and 30% stocks. This asset allocation would be appropriate, because at this point you are entering the liquidation period for the investment program, and you would not want to take much risk.

Whether the investment program is for pre-retirement, retirement, or for college savings, for all the reasons discussed above—automatic asset allocation, use of index funds, low management fees—target funds are the investment of choice. There are other ways to manage these kinds of investment programs, but most of them will do worse, and maybe much worse, in helping you to achieve your objectives for them.

Bottom Line

- The first step in designing a long-term investment program is to develop a lifetime asset allocation plan that has a high equity exposure at the beginning and that gradually increases the bond exposure and reduces the stock exposure until the end of the plan, when there is a high exposure to bonds.
- This lifetime asset allocation plan integrates the pre-retirement period and the post-retirement period into a continuum, so that you transfer naturally from one to the other.
- Balanced funds do not give you the long-term asset allocation pattern that you need.
- Target date funds provide a number of significant advantages over other alternatives. Some, but not all, of these funds use index funds; they all change the asset allocation over time, and some have very low cost.
- The Vanguard Target Fund 2045, for example, provides all of the advantages of Target Funds in general, including index funds and low fees, and, in particular, its asset allocation over time matches very closely what is a reasonable lifetime asset allocation plan.
- What this means is that you can use just one vehicle to accomplish all of your objectives for both the pre-retirement and post-retirement periods and effectively put your investment plan on a well-designed and well-implemented autopilot.
- This approach is by far the best thing you can do to achieve your objectives. Anything else runs a very considerable risk of doing worse rather than better.
- Immediate fixed annuities may have a place in your retirement planning, depending on how concerned you are about income security for a portion of your retirement expenses.

- There is a variety of college savings plans, including 529 plans, Coverdell Education Savings Accounts, and Uniform Gifts (or Transfers) to Minors accounts.
- 529 plans have considerable advantages over the other plans, and they should be funded as aggressively as is consistent with all the other priorities, including contributions to 401(k) plans and Pay Yourself First.
- As is the case for long-term retirement planning, target date funds should be the investments of choice for 529 plans.

PART VI

Documents

Chapter 12

Creating the Necessary Documents for the Management of Your Life

The secret of all victory lies in the organization of the
non-obvious.

Marcus Aurelius
Roman Emperor

In this chapter, I will discuss three important categories of critical documents
and outline why it is essential that they be created:

- Basic background information about you and your family
- Wills, trusts, guardians, powers of attorney, and letters of
  instruction
- Special documents related to health care

Basic Background Information

Most of us have a variety of personal background information in
unorganized and scattered records. In general, we think we know where
things are or might be found, but it is surprising in many cases how long
it takes to recover some important piece of personal information. At such
times, we resolve to get better organized, but usually not much happens until

179

the next episode. I think this is because people do not believe that getting basic background information organized has a high priority.

This situation is not much satisfaction to anyone (spouse, children, and professionals who provide services to you, such as lawyers) who might have to access this information suddenly. I think you have an obligation to yourself and to others who might have to act on your behalf to have your affairs in good order all the time.

Like so many other activities discussed in this book, a significant amount of effort is required to collect and list all the necessary personal information. Fortunately, however, after the initial setup, the work required to maintain your information is relatively modest. I think you will find that the payoff for the work you do will make it worthwhile. Furthermore, it should add to the feeling, which I hope you have developed from reading this book and implementing its recommendations, that you are in control of all the financial aspects of your life.

Contacts

The first thing that someone you authorize to act on your behalf will want to know is who the important contacts are and how to get in touch with them. The following should be included in this list:

- Names and addresses of key family members (e.g., spouse, children, mother and father).
- Your principal doctors, including your general practitioner and any specialists for particular medical problems you may have.
- Names, addresses, and telephone numbers of professional advisers, including lawyer, tax accountant, financial planner, stock broker, and insurance agent, if any.
- The name, address, and telephone number of the person who is in charge of human resources at the company for which you work. This person will be able to provide complete information about your benefits, in case that information is not recorded someplace else.

Financial Accounts

Create a list of financial accounts that will provide ready access to important financial information about you and your family. This list should include the following information:

- The latest family balance sheet, as developed in chapter 5. This is the best place to start, because it should show all of your assets and liabilities.
- For each of the assets shown in the family balance sheet, the name of the asset, the institution that is involved, if any, your account number, and the name, address, and telephone number of the contact person at the institution involved with the asset.
- For each of the liabilities shown in the family balance sheet, the name of the liability (e.g., mortgage, car loan), the institution that is involved, if any, your account number, and the name, address, and telephone number of the contact person at the institution involved with the liability.
- All insurance policies, including the names of the insurance companies and the policy numbers.

Location of Important Personal Documents

Having the information about the nature of assets and liabilities is a good start, but it is also necessary to identify the location of these and other key financial items. In many cases, necessary actions with respect to them cannot take place without having the original documents or copies. The locations for these documents, which would include your safe deposit box, your safe at home, and your lawyer's office, should be listed:

- All assets and liabilities
- Employee benefit information, particularly the annual statement provided by your employer, if any
- Life and other insurance policies
- Birth certificate
- Marriage license
- The original of your will. In this case, a copy will not do. Without the original, your estate may not be distributed as you had intended. Many people keep the original will at the office of the lawyer who helped create it.
- Other estate planning documents
- Health care proxy, living will, and powers of attorney (see below)
- The forms naming beneficiaries for your retirement accounts. In general, retirement accounts pass to the beneficiaries based on the beneficiary designations and not based on the will. Therefore, it is exceedingly important to consider carefully whom you want

your beneficiaries to be and to make sure that the retirement plan custodians have written documentation from you indicating your decisions.

Wills, Trusts, Guardians, Powers of Attorney, and Letters of Instruction

Wills

One of the most important documents for yourself or your family is a will. The simple reason is that, without a will, your assets will not necessarily go to those you would like to have them. Rather, you will be deemed to have died intestate (that is, without a will), and your assets will be distributed according to the laws of the state in which you live.

A will is not a complicated document to create, and it can be modified or rewritten entirely as circumstances change. A will is a formal way of expressing your wishes about the disposition of your assets on your death that is recognized by each state. In the case of a family, there should be a will for both husband and wife. You will also have to name an executor, who has the responsibility of literally "executing" your will, which means implementing all the provisions of your will as you have defined them.

Trusts

There are all kinds of trusts for all kinds of reasons, and they are usually provided by a lawyer who specializes in trusts and estates. This can be a very complicated field, and it is not my purpose here to go into depth about trusts.

However, there are clearly situations in which simple trusts are necessary and easily understood. The following are some examples:

- Under the terms of your will, you would normally leave most of your assets to your spouse. However, what happens if the spouse is not qualified to manage the assets? In this case, you should create a trust to manage and distribute the assets to your spouse and any minor children. There is a great deal of flexibility in creating and operating a trust so that your objectives for it can be met.

- If you have minor children, it is necessary to determine what you would want to happen to your assets if you had no spouse and you were to suddenly pass away or, in the case of a couple, both husband and wife were to pass away simultaneously. At least until the age of majority, if not much longer, the children would not be in a position to manage the assets properly, and you should create a trust to manage and distribute the assets to the children under terms that you specify. In this case, you can specify how long you want the trust to operate and when it should be paid out to the beneficiaries.

- If you have a child who is disabled, you had no spouse, and you were to pass away suddenly, or, in the case of a couple, both husband and wife were to pass away simultaneously, you would want to create a special trust for this person, which is independent of everything else you are doing, to make sure that the lifetime needs of this person are properly addressed.

In each of these cases, you would have to name a trustee to oversee the trust, usually a representative of a fiduciary institution, your lawyer, a member of your family, or a trusted friend.

Whenever you set up a trust, it is a good idea to prepare a letter of instruction to the trustee in which you spell out the purposes of the trust and how you expect it to be managed.

Guardians

Guardians are primarily of concern for minor children, although you can see that in the third case mentioned above, you might want the guardianship to last longer than the achievement of majority.

Guardians, by definition, are responsible for the physical well-being of those for whom they are guardians. Therefore, you have to choose guardians whom you think will provide for your children in a way and in an environment that is as close as possible to what you would have provided. It is imperative that you have a very candid discussion with possible guardians prior to their appointment to determine if this is the case. It would be a good idea to have a letter of understanding signed by you and the guardian regarding what you would like to have for your children.

Guardians are clearly not the same thing as trustees, and it might make sense to be sure that they are different. For example, if you and your spouse were to pass away in a common disaster, you might want to name a relative as guardian of your children. However, a good guardian would not necessarily be a good trustee, and you might want to ask someone else to be the trustee of the trust you have set up for their benefit.

Powers of Attorney

A power of attorney (POA) is a legal document in which you give authorization to someone you trust to take legal action on your behalf and to manage your affairs if you are unable to do so yourself. The person granting the POA is generally called the principal, and the person to whom the POA is granted is called the attorney-in-fact.

The principal may grant limited or broad legal authority, and the POA is frequently used in cases of disability or illness or in cases in which the principal cannot be present to execute legal documents. There are several different kinds of POAs:

- Nondurable—this is a POA designed for a specific transaction, like a real estate closing, or for handling the principal's financial affairs while he or she is out of the country.
- Durable—this is a POA that allows the attorney-in-fact to act for the principal in all matters, including when the principal is physically incapable of making decisions. It is in effect until revoked by the principal.
- Springing—this is a POA that literally springs into effect as a result of certain specified developments primarily having to do with illness or disability.

Clearly, the nondurable power has limited application to specific and anticipated events. The springing POA sounds like a good idea at first, but in the end it is difficult to implement because it is hard to specify exactly what circumstances cause it to "spring" and how to obtain medical approval that those circumstances actually exist. The durable POA is the most generally useful, because it is always there and covers the broadest range of circumstances that might require a POA.

Since the POA grants extraordinary authority to one person, it is obviously critical to choose someone as attorney-in-fact who is completely trustworthy. Creating a POA requires weighing the broad authority of the attorney-in-fact against the need to have a person who can act in your best interests if you cannot. In my opinion, the need for the latter outweighs the risk of the former.

Letter of Instruction

This is a letter you write to the people you have chosen to care for your affairs and your family after you pass away; the list should include the following:

- Your choices for funeral arrangements
- General comments to the guardians of your minor children about how you would like them to be raised
- General comments to trustees of any trusts, beyond the strict terms of the trust, concerning how you would like the trusts to be managed

Special Documents Related to Health Care

There are two important documents related to your health care that you should create. These are not very pleasant to think about, but they are necessary to make sure that your wishes for the type of care you want to receive are honored.

- Living will—this is a document in which you indicate how you want to be treated if you are suffering from any of the following conditions: (1) terminal condition, (2) permanent coma, and (3) persistent vegetative state. For these conditions, you will specify whether you wish to receive: (1) artificial life support, (2) artificially administered food and water, and (3) basic care to reduce pain and suffering.

- Medical power of attorney (sometimes called a health care proxy)— this is a POA like those described above, only this one is specifically designed to authorize someone to make health care decisions on your behalf when you are unable to make them. Unlike some of the other POAs, this one might be granted primarily to a family member or a close friend with whom you have reviewed your wishes and your living will.

The whole field of living wills and medical powers of attorney is undergoing considerable change in terms of how they are supposed to function. Furthermore, different states have different forms and requirements, and doctors may have their own interpretations of the meaning of living wills, given their responsibilities to preserve life. This is why it is critical to have carefully drawn forms that properly reflect your wishes and a carefully selected individual with a medical power of attorney to make sure that they are followed.

Bottom Line

- For your benefit and the benefit of others who may have to act on the information, it is essential to take the time and make the investment to organize and maintain your personal information. This includes contact information, information about assets and liabilities, and the locations of important personal financial documents.
- You must create a will to dispose of your assets as you want them distributed and to define other arrangements. Otherwise, you will die intestate, and your assets will be distributed under the laws of the state in which you live.
- It is imperative to create trusts and assign guardians for minor children in the case in which parents pass away.
- There may be circumstances in which you will be unable to act on your behalf, and in this case you should create a durable power of attorney and give it to someone you can trust to act for you.
- Every person should have a living will, which specifies the health care with which you want to be provided under certain circumstances, and give a medical power of attorney to a person whom you trust to make sure that your wishes regarding your health care are followed.
- Create letters of instruction to convey to those you have chosen to manage your affairs and be guardians of minor children your wishes for their discretionary activities on your behalf.

Conclusion

The title of this book, *You Can Do It*, could easily have been *You Must Do It*. You will not achieve your long-term objectives unless you make the investment to get the key aspects of your financial affairs in order and as much on autopilot as possible. As I have mentioned several times, a personal investment is necessary to get to this point in each case, but after the initial investment, you are in charge, and maintenance is relatively easy. Contrast this approach with the alternative, which is to struggle along, going from crisis to crisis, and never being in control.

- Get your financial affairs in order by starting with setting objectives. Without clearly defined objectives, you will never really know why you are doing what you are doing and whether you have accomplished anything while you are doing it.
- Put your cash management on autopilot, so that you know where your money is going. Your bills will get paid, your credit rating may improve, and you will earn as much as you can on any extra cash.
- Organize and regularly update your personal balance sheet, listing your assets, liabilities, and personal net worth. The change in

your personal net worth over time is probably the most significant demonstration of the progress you are making toward achieving your long-term goals.

- Construct a budget at the beginning of each year based on the spending categories that are important to you and on your take home income, track how you are doing relative to budget in each of these categories and overall, and maintain a firm discipline to stay within the budgeted amounts for each category. Unlike the U.S. government, you cannot print money. Excess spending will inevitably end up in very expensive (reverse compounding) credit card debt.

- Make certain that you have all the necessary personal, property, and liability insurance coverages, so that you can protect yourself and the personal net worth you are working so hard to build.

- Determine the level of income you will need in retirement, what amount of assets will provide that level of retirement income, and what investment program to put in place that will give you the best chance of providing the assets you will need.

- Take the time to create a set of critical documents that will enable you to control how your assets are used, how your minor children are raised if you are not around, and how you want to be treated in the event of an incapacitating illness or death.

This book is designed to be an integrated whole. You should resist the temptation to take action in one area and not in the others. In an important sense, actions with respect to the subjects covered in his book are equally important, and not addressing them all will leave you with a gap somewhere that could turn out to be critically important. I hope you will find that this book deserves to be in the third category of books, as defined above by Sir Francis Bacon.

I am convinced that you will find that the effort to get yourself into control of your financial affairs and to maintain that control will be one of the most rewarding efforts of your life. However, the clock is ticking, and delaying making that effort can turn out to be very costly. The most important thing to keep in mind is that

YOU CAN DO IT!

Notes

Chapter 2

1. John Brynjolfsson, portfolio manager of the Pimco Real Return fund, the *New York Times*, June 17, 2007, B6
2. Stocks, Bonds, Bills, and Inflation 2007 Yearbook, Morningstar, Inc., Chicago, Illinois
3. Ibid.
4. Ibid.
5. Ibid.
6. Ibid.

Chapter 4

1. The *Wall Street Journal*, April 12, 2007, C2
2. *USA Today* (sometime in July, 2007)
3. The *Wall Street Journal*, July 18, 2007 , D5

Chapter 6

1. *Business Week*, March 12, 2007, 13
2. The *Wall Street Journal*, May 4, 2007, A12

3.   Ibid., March 15, 2007, D1

Chapter 8

1.   Employee Benefit Research Institute (EBRI), 2006 Retirement Confidence Survey, April 4, 2006
2.   Ibid.
3.   Fidelity Research Institute 2007 Retirement Index, Fidelity Research Institute, March 12, 2007
4.   Ibid.
5.   EBRI Data Book on Employee Benefits, Chapter 11: "Retirement Plan Finances." Table 11.3 (updated February 2007) "Nominal and Real Private Trusteed Pension Assets—Total Nominal and Real Assets of Private Trusteed Pension Plans, by Plan Type and Asset Type, Year-end, 1995–2004"
6.   Ibid., Chapter 10, Table 10.4. "Aggregate Trends in Defined Benefit and Defined Contribution Retirement Plan Sponsorship, Participation, and Vesting" (updated September 2002). "Primary Plan Active Participants Trends by Plan Size—Active Participants in Primary Defined Benefit and Defined Contribution Plans, Selected Years, 1985–1998"
7.   U.S. Department of Labor, Bureau of Labor Statistics, Bureau of Labor Statistics Data, December 27, 2006

Chapter 9

7.   *EBRI News*, July 20, 2006
2.   "EBRI Issue Brief No. 296," August 2006
3.   Federal Trade Commission, "Facts for Consumers"
4.   2007 *Wall Street Journal* Financial Planning Survey, the *Wall Street Journal* October 6–7, R7

Chapter 10

1.   "Vanguard U.S. Government Bond Funds Annual Report," January 31, 2007, 7
2.   Ibid., page 5
3.   John Bogle, *The Little Book of Common Sense Investing*, 33
4.   Ibid., 127
5.   Ibid.

6. The *Wall Street Journal*, July 12, 2007, C13
7. The *Wall Street Journal*, May 7, 2007, R1
8. John Bogle, *The Little Book of Common Sense Investing*, 174

Chapter 11

1. The *Wall Street Journal*, May 10, 2007, D6
2. www.Vanguard.com, accessed April 12, 2007
3. Ibid.
4. Ibid.
5. Vanguard Target Retirement Funds Prospectus, 1/31/07, page 50
6. The *Wall Street Journal*, 7/9/07, page R3
7. Ibid., July 14–15, 2007, R3
8. Ibid., June 15, 2007, A14
9. Ibid.
10. Ibid., July 14–15, 2007, R3

Index

Note: Page numbers followed by "*f*" are references to a figure on the designated page.

equity mutual funds, 151
exchange traded funds (ETFs), 152–153
executor of will, 182
Experian, 58

F

FICO, credit measurement scale, 58
Fidelity Research Institute, 110
financial accounts, 181
financial management. *See* cash management
financial planners, role of, 98, 110, 172
fixed annuities, 171
fixed income assets, 169
fixed income mutual funds, 148–149
Foley, Jay, 88
formal objectives, setting of, 34
fund manager, role of, 161
funeral arrangements, 185

G

gift taxes, 173–174
Government National Mortgage Association (GNMA), 149, 150
gross income, 76
"guaranteed renewable" disability insurance, 102
guardians, 184

H

health care documents, 186
health care proxy, 186
health insurance, 95–96
    cafeteria plans, 95
    dental and vision coverage, 96
    drug plan, 96
    employers' role, 95
    HDHP/HSA, 96
    types of, 95–96
health savings accounts (HSAs), 96
high deductible health plans (HDHPs), 96

home equity loans, 67, 69, 87
home ownership, 17
house, insuringi
    dwelling insurance, 102–103
    insurance companies and, 104
    liability insurance, 103

I

immediate annuity, 171
implicit objectives, setting of, 34–35
income deposits, 47–48, 48*f*
income taxes, 166
index funds, 152
individual investors, 150
individual stocks, 150–151
inflation-protected securities, 165–166
in-network coverage plans, 95
institutional investors, 150
insurance
    deductible amount and, 102–103
    health (*see* health insurance)
    overall liability, 94
    overview of, 105–106
    personal, 94 (*see also* personal insurance)
    property, 94
    purchase options for, 106
    tips for purchasing, 93–94
investment programs. *See also* long-term investment program
    basic asset classes and, 13–14
    expected return rates for bonds and stocks, 146–148
    investment alternatives for bonds and stocks (*See* bonds; stocks)
investment returns
    and basic assets, 13
    definition of, 14
investment time horizon, 161, 174

L

letter of instruction, 185

Printed in the United States
209663BV00004B/10-36/P